TOP 10 ⭐ Sierra Espuña

The pine-clad mountain range of the Sierra Espuña erupts magically from the parched Murcian plain. A regional park since 1995, it offers spectacular walking and mountain-biking trails, with some tougher hikes across the peaks. To the east lie the "bad lands", an unearthly swathe of arid hills and abrupt canyons, and scattered across the park's northern flanks are the ancient snow wells, picturesque ruins deep in the pine forest.

1 Pozos de Nieve

These strange, circular brick huts were used to store snow, which was packed into ice, and transported by donkey to the towns to make ice cream. They were used from the 16th century right up until the 1920s.

Sierra Espuña

PARK GUIDE

The best way to get to the Sierra Espuña is from Alhama de Murcia, as this road passes the Visitor Centre, where you can pick up maps and information. The snow wells are found in the northwest of the park; take the road signposted *pozos de nieve* from the Collado Bermejo viewing point, and walk down the path near the car park.

2 Visitor Centre

This handsomely restored building contains a small but lively exhibition geared towards children, outlining the park's history and the wildlife to be found within its borders. An information desk has maps and leaflets with details of walking trails.

3 Flora and Fauna

The indigenous forest has been substantially supplemented by pine. You may well see bats, mouflon – a wild sheep (left) – and wild boar; mountain cats are less common.

Previous pages Catedral de Santa María, Murcia

4 Peaks
Thrusting up through verdant forest, the stony peaks of the Sierra Espuña **(below)** are a magnificent sight. There are more than 20 peaks over 1,000 m (3,280 ft), with 1,583-m (5,194-ft) Espuña being the highest. Pedro López (1,507 m/4,944 ft) is also pretty spectacular.

7 Barrancos de Gebas
At the eastern end of the park is the strange lunar landscape of the Barrancos de Gebas, known as the *tierras malas* ("bad lands"), where the lush sierra gives way to a series of arid ravines and gullies **(above)**.

8 Miradors
The park has a series of *miradors* (viewing points), with stunning views over peaks, forest and riverbeds. The finest views are from Espuña and the Morrón Chico.

10 Drive
The drive through the Sierra Espuña is extraordinary; the road twists up through the Collado Bermejo, offering a staggering panorama of jutting crags and plunging valleys, then down again through flower-strewn woodland to the Visitor Centre.

5 Birds
The park is rich in bird life, particularly raptors, among them golden, booted and Bonelli's eagles, eagle and tawny owls, peregrine falcons, goshawks and hawk owls.

9 Alhama de Murcia
Alhama de Murcia is not the loveliest town in the area, but it's the easiest access point for the park, and a good place to buy supplies or find a hotel.

6 Walking and Mountain-Biking Trails
The park is full of superb walking and biking trails geared toward visitors of all levels **(below)**. Choose from simple woodland paths, suitable for families, to tougher routes across the peaks. The information points provide maps and leaflets.

NEED TO KNOW
MAP L3

Visitor Centre (Centro Ricardo Cordoníu): Parque Regional de Sierra Espuña; 968 43 14 30 (information and park refuge/camp site booking line); open Jun–Sep: 8:30am–3:30pm daily; Oct–May: 9am–2pm & 3–5:30pm daily; www. sierraespuna.com

■ Fuente del Hilo is an inexpensive café-restaurant located near the Visitor Centre. It dishes up grilled local meat and fish 623 30 88 12; closed Mon, Tue & Aug).

■ There are three camping areas and, for serious hikers, four mountain refuges in the park *(see p131)*. The Visitor Centre has information about these and can provide details of the best hotels, *pensiones* and *casas rurales* in the region.

🔟 ⭐ Hort del Cura, Elx (Elche)

Elx, a tranquil city at the centre of a vast plain, is surrounded by a lush palm grove, first established by the Phoenicians in the 7th century BC and today a UNESCO World Heritage Site. In one corner of this grove is the stunning Hort del Cura (Priest's Garden), with more than 700 palms and a blaze of brilliant blooms around a restful pond. First laid out in its current form in the 19th century by Don José Castaño (the priest after whom it is named), the garden achieved international fame in the 1940s under Juan Orts Román.

1 Imperial Palm
Named in honour of a visit by the Empress of Austria in 1894, this majestic palm is almost 200 years old. With seven huge branches, it weighs around eight tonnes.

The spectacular palms of the Hort del Cura, Elx

2 Sculptures
The most dramatic sculpture in the park is by Alicantino artist Eusebio Sempere – a gently revolving circle of metal spikes that appears to shift shape as it turns (above).

3 La Casa
The simple house at the park's entrance was built in 1940, and incorporates palm trunks into its design. It holds administrative offices and isn't open to the public.

4 Date Palms
Most of the palms in Elx are date palms. The story goes that they came here with the Phoenicians, who ate the dates on the long sea journey, and then planted the stones.

5 Flowers
The Hort de Cura is full of strelitzias, better known as "birds of paradise" plants for their spiky forms and extraordinary colours. There's also a brilliant tumble of purple and red bougainvillea at the southwestern end of the garden.

Hort del Cura

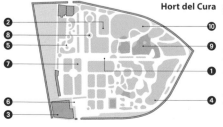

8 Bust of Jaime I
A small bust of King Jaime I sits at the western end of the park **(left)**, commemorating the king's decision to save the palm groves of Elx from destruction after the city was taken from the Arabs in 1265.

9 Lily Pond
Turtles bask in the sun and frogs chatter on the fringes of the charming lily pond at the very heart of the park. You can make your own way across it on a series of stepping stones.

ELX PALMS

About 95 per cent of the palms in Elx are date palms, which produce vast quantities of fruit. While some of the fruit is cultivated and sold, the most economically viable part of the palms are the dried fronds. Elx is the main supplier of fronds to make crosses for use on Palm Sunday. The palm crosses are often kept all year round because they are popularly believed to ward off lightning.

10 Rock Garden and Cactuses
Behind the pond, rocks form a Wild West-style backdrop to the cactus collection **(above)**. There are tall, spiky cactuses as big as trees, many sprouting scarlet fruit and flowers, as well as plump varieties of the type known as "mother-in-law's cushion".

6 Chapel
A tiny chapel holds the remains of Juan Orts Román, who remodelled the gardens in the 1940s and ensured that they received international attention. Román was the son of the *cura* (priest) after whom the gardens are named.

7 Named Palms
Since 1900, a number of palms have been dedicated to distinguished people, and bear a small plaque. The dedicatees are sent the fruits of the tree during their lifetime.

NEED TO KNOW

MAP D6, Q1

Hort del Cura: C/Porta de la Morera 49; 965 45 19 36; check website for hours; adm €5 (children €3); www.huertodelcura.com

Elx tourist office: Plaza del Parque 3; 966 65 81 96; open 9am–7pm Mon–Fri & 10am–7pm Sat (6pm Nov–Mar), 10am–2pm Sun & public hols

■ There is a kiosk selling drinks and snacks within the garden. For a smart lunch, make your way to the elegant hotel Huerto del Cura directly opposite the garden at Porta de la Morera (966 61 00 11).

■ The small gardens are best visited early in the morning or late in the evening, when the crowds are smaller. Come out of season if you can, and try to avoid weekends. There is a useful audioguide to help you make the most of your visit.

TOP10 ★ Isla Tabarca

Tabarca is the only inhabited island on Alicante's coast. The eastern end is wild and empty, guarded by an 18th-century watchtower and a remote lighthouse; at the western end is the pretty walled village of Nova Tabarca. The island's only sandy beach, with a cluster of cafés and restaurants, backs onto the port. It can get very busy in summer, especially at weekends. The clear waters surrounding the island are a marine reserve and popular with divers and snorkellers.

Isla Tabarca

Isla Tabarca

3 Casa del Gobernador

Long since stripped of its original fittings, the 18th-century Governor's House is now a charming small hotel *(see p127)*. It remains the grandest residence on the island.

1 Lighthouse

Tabarca's lighthouse emerges from the scrubby wilderness at the eastern tip of the island. It is a substantial 19th-century building combining sturdy living quarters with a slender tower. The lighthouse is not open to the public but is a pretty spot to walk to.

2 Iglesia de San Pedro y San Pablo

Dedicated to St Peter and St Paul, Nova Tabarca's appealing little church, perched right above the crystal blue sea, is built of faded, rosy stone **(right)**. Its simple façade has some very appealing Baroque flourishes.

⑦ Torre de San José

This 18th-century watchtower was part of the fortifications that defended the island against pirate raids. In the 19th century it was a prison **(above)**.

⑧ Beach

The main beach **(left)**, a small arc of sand opposite the port, is full of visitors in summer. The gorgeous coves, which fringe the island with their shingle beaches, are less crowded.

⑨ City Walls

The 18th-century village of Nova Tabarca was fortified against pirates. Stretches of wall and some gates survive.

⑩ Nova Tabarca

The streets of this simple village with low, brightly painted houses offer delightful glimpses of flower-filled patios and shaded squares **(below)**.

④ The Islands

Tabarca is the largest island of a small archipelago. The islets off its coast are perfect for swimming.

⑤ Marine Reserve

Declared a marine reserve in 1986, Tabarca's waters contain a wealth of aquatic life among the reefs. Several companies in Santa Pola offer diving and snorkelling trips.

⑥ Port

Tabarca's port is the island's hub. A few colourful fishing boats are dwarfed by the incoming and outgoing ferries.

NEED TO KNOW

MAP E6, R1

Santa Pola Tourist Office: C/Astilleros 4; 966 69 60 52

■ There are several places to eat in the port area, offering local specialities such as *caldero tabarquino*, a delicious fish stew. However, prices are high, so consider stocking up on snacks before coming.

■ The ferry service from Santa Pola (with five crossings in a week and six at weekends) is faster and more frequent than the service from Alicante (three times daily in summer and once a day for the rest of the year). There are regular crossings from Benidorm or Dénia in the summer.

■ Companies offering diving and snorkelling trips include Anthias (Club Nautico de Santa Pola, Pantalán 6, Santa Pola; www.anthias.es); and Dive Academy Santa Pola (Puerto Deportivo 2, Marina Miramar, Local 3, Santa Pola; 966 69 90 88; www.diveacademy-santapola.com).

TOP10 ⭐ Palau Ducal, Gandia (Gandía)

This impressive Gothic palace with late 13th-century origins was acquired by the Dukes of Borja – better known by their Italian name Borgia – in the late 15th century. It was expanded over the years, and its most lavish apartments date from the late 18th century, when Baroque salons dripping with gold leaf were added. Famous for the ceramic tiles adorning its walls, galleries and balconies, the palace has been restored immaculately by its current owners, the Jesuits.

1 Exhibition
The history of the palace and the story of the Borja family are recounted in a fun exhibition at the beginning of the tour **(below)**. Note the glowing *azulejos* (tiles), which adorn the walls of the projection room – there are even finer tiles within the palace itself.

2 Entrance Hall
Nothing survives of the 13th-century palace but the entrance hall, which leads on to the central patio. The beamed ceiling is original but its painted decoration has faded over the centuries.

3 Salón de Coronas
The majestic 16th-century Hall of Crowns takes its name from the crowns that decorate the elaborate wooden ceiling **(above)**. One of the building's oldest windows can be found in this room.

4 Galería Dorada
The sumptuous 18th-century Galería Dorada, a succession of apartments opening into one long hall, is a breathtaking whirl of gilded stucco and colourful tiles.

5 Chapel
A brilliant blue vaulted ceiling with golden stars soars above the Neo-Gothic chapel, created in the room that was formerly St Francis of Borja's office **(below)**.

ST FRANCIS OF BORJA (1510–72)

Francis of Borja was an advisor to Carlos I of Spain at the time of the queen's death in 1539. Asked to escort her remains for burial in Granada, Francis was so appalled at the sight of her decomposed body that he announced his intention to "follow a master who cannot die" and abandoned the court for a religious life. He joined the Jesuits in 1548, and was finally canonised in 1670.

⑦ Main Façade

The simple stone façade, a sober Gothic portal topped with a faded coat of arms and flanked by narrow windows, gives no hint of the luxury within (above).

First floor of the Palau Ducal

❶ (on ground floor)

⑥ Oratory

A simple chapel next to St Francis of Borja's humble bedroom was transformed in the 19th century into this miniature oratory with a series of murals and an exquisite marquetry floor.

⑧ Patio de Armas

Carriages used to clatter over the Patio de Armas, the main courtyard of the old palace, when making for the stables at its northeastern corner.

⑩ Salón de Águilas

This extravagantly decorated 18th-century hall exhibits a dazzling gilded frieze of fierce *águilas* (eagles) feasting on clumps of fruit.

⑨ The Four Elements

The Galería Dorada features a stunning mosaic reflecting the four elements; the sun (fire) is encircled by birds (air), fish (water) and flowers (earth).

NEED TO KNOW

MAP F2 ■ C/Duc Alfons el Vell 1 ■ 962 87 14 65 ■ www. palauducal.com

Open 10am–1:30pm, 4–7:30pm Mon–Sat (Oct–Mar: 10am–1:30pm & 3–6:15pm), 10am–1:15pm Sun. Guided tours are available at 11am, noon, 4 & 5pm Mon–Sat

(Apr–Oct: also at 6pm), 11am & noon Sun. Night tours: Jul & Aug: 8:30pm daily (by reservation only); Audioguides are available at €2; Adm €7 (children €4)

■ Nearby, the Telero restaurant, which overlooks a garden, offers modern Mediterranean

fare (Carrer Sant Ponç 7; 962 867 318; closed Mon, Sun & D).

■ Full access to the palace is by guided tour only. Tours are given in either Spanish or Valencian. Call ahead to ensure that the multimedia exhibit can be heard in your language.

TOP 10 ⭐ Catedral de Santa María, Murcia

The Cathedral of Santa María looms proudly over the centre of Murcia. The finest Baroque building in a city overflowing with Baroque architecture, it also contains some fine examples of the Gothic and Renaissance styles. The first stone was laid on the site of a former Arab mosque in 1394, and the first mass was celebrated in the mid-15th century. The richly ornamented façade was added in the 18th century.

Baroque Façade ①
The main façade **(right)**, with its Corinthian columns and lavishly carved stonework, was built between 1739 and 1754 by architect Jaime Bort. It overlooks the lovely Plaza del Cardenal Belluga.

② Altar Mayor
The vast main altarpiece **(above)** was partly rebuilt in 1862 by a Yecla sculptor. It forms an impressive golden wall behind the main altar.

③ Coro
The sumptuous wooden choir stalls in the Gothic-style choir are densely carved with an array of scenes taken from the Bible.

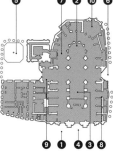

Catedral de Santa María

NEED TO KNOW

MAP U6, N3

Catedral de Santa María:
Plaza del Cardenal Belluga; 968 21 63 44; open 7am–1pm daily (until 2pm Sun) & 5–8pm Mon–Fri, 5–9pm Sat & 6:30–9:30pm Sun

Museo de la Catedral: open 10am–5pm Tue–Sat, 10am–1pm Sun; adm €3, tours €5, under 25s €4

■ A short walk away, Los Zagales (C/Polo de Medina 4; 968 21 55 79; closed Sun) is a great place for tapas, and is popular with locals. The walls are covered with photographs of famous footballers and bullfighters.

■ Bring €1 coins to light up the cathedral interior, such as the Choir, the Capilla de los Vélez and the Capilla del Junterón.

④ Puerta del Perdón
Surmounted by an exquisite sculpture of the Virgin Mary being attended by angels, the central doorway of the main façade was once reserved for royalty.

5 Bell Tower

The delightful bell tower, with its Baroque frills and flounces, is an oddly harmonious mishmash of styles.

7 Puerta de la Sacristía

Baroque at its most flamboyant, this extravagant doorway is in the form of a splendid triumphal arch, with columns and pedestals supporting a host of cherubs surmounted by the three Virtues.

THE BELL TOWER

Work started on the cathedral bell tower in 1519, but it was not completed until 1793. Each of its five levels is in a different style. Starting with a theatrical Gothic section complete with swarms of fabulous creatures, the tower ascends to a winsome Baroque lantern right at the very top. You can climb the bell tower; access is through the Museo de la Catedral.

9 Museo de la Catedral

The cathedral museum includes paintings, sculptures and ceremonial objects, including an extraordinary Baroque silver monstrance.

6 Puerta de los Apóstoles

The intricate Gothic portal on the southern side of the cathedral **(below)** is set in a sea of sculpture, including images of the apostles and a cloud of angelic musicians. Queen Isabella's coat of arms caps the portal – she gave generously toward the cathedral's construction.

8 Capilla del Junterón

This dazzling chapel (another aristocratic burial place) is the grandest expression of Renaissance architecture in Murcia. Adorned with saints and Classical figures, it contains a splendid 16th-century altarpiece topped by a spectacular relief.

10 Capilla de los Vélez

The jewel of the building is the Capilla de los Vélez **(above)**, the magnificent late-15th-century burial place of the immensely powerful Marquises of Vélez. Look out for the "noble savages" – a fashionable motif after Christopher Columbus's voyage to the Americas.

The Top 10 of Everything

Moros y Cristianos festival in the village of Alcoi (Alcoy)

Moments in History

Engraving of the First Punic War

1 Prehistory

The slither of Spain's southeast coastline that forms the Costa Blanca has been inhabited since Paleolithic times. Iberian settlements began to appear around 3000 BC, hence the name Iberian Peninsula. Later, two Bronze Age cultures emerged: Argaric in the south and Valencian in the north.

2 Phoenicians, Greeks and Carthaginians

By 1000 BC, the Phoenicians and the Greeks were establishing trading settlements along the coast. The Carthaginians, landless after their defeat in the First Punic War, established Carthage in the 3rd century BC.

3 Romans and Visigoths

Rome crushed Carthage and renamed the city as Carthago Nova (modern-day Cartagena) in the Second Punic War, marking the beginning of Roman domination. The Romans named the land Hispania and established important settlements at Dénia (Denia), Alicante (Alacant) and Cartagena. The fall of the Western Roman Empire in AD 476 left Hispania in the hands of the Visigoths, a nomadic Germanic tribe who arrived in AD 411. However, dynastic disputes left them ripe for conquest by the next wave of invaders.

4 Arabs

In 711, the Amazigh from Africa invaded the Iberian Peninsula, renaming it as Al-Andalus. This territory was ruled first by a mighty caliphate and then as a series of smaller *taifas* (kingdoms), which included Valencia. Arabic irrigation techniques created the orchards that still characterize the Costa Blanca today.

5 The Reconquista

Pockets of northern Spain resisted the Arab armies, and it was from here that the Christian Reconquest was launched. Battles raged through much of the 13th century. Murcia (Mursiya) was taken by Jaime I of Aragón in 1266; Alicante (Al-Lekant) fell to Jaime II in 1296.

6 The Kingdom of Valencia

After the Reconquest, Jaime I re-established the Kingdom of Valencia, with special privileges, including its own currency. These were only withdrawn after Valencia backed the losing side in the War of the Spanish Succession (1700–1714).

Illustration of the Second Punic War

7 Murcia on the Frontier

In 1244, Murcia, which bordered the Arabic kingdom of Granada, became part of the Kingdom of Castile. When Granada fell in 1492, Muslim converts poured into Murcia.

8 The Lost Years

Spain suffered during the wars and political upheavals of the 18th and 19th centuries. Simmering unrest in the early years of the 20th century erupted into the bloody Civil War (1936–9), won by General Franco.

General Franco reviewing troops

9 Franco's Dictatorship

Regional differences, including the Valencian language, were savagely suppressed under Franco's dictatorship. The advent of mass tourism in the 1960s brought jobs, money and much new development. Franco died in 1975, and democracy was restored.

10 Costa Blanca Today

In reaction to decades of brutally enforced centralized power, Spain's regions clamoured for devolution. Valencia, which comprises the Costa Blanca, became one of Spain's 17 autonomous regions in 1982. The 1990s saw economic growth, but the 2008 global financial crisis hit hard, and Costa Blanca was no exception. Despite a thriving tourist industry, the region's economy is still slowly recovering, resulting in factionalism.

TOP 10 HISTORICAL FIGURES

1 Dama de Elx (4th century BC)
The origins of this exquisite Iberian sculpture are shrouded in mystery *(see p91)*. No one knows if the woman depicted was mythical or a real person.

2 Hannibal Barca (c. 247–c.183 BC)
The formidable Carthaginian military general who famously crossed the Alps with elephants at the start of the Second Punic War.

3 Abd al-Rahman II (792–852)
The Emir of Córdoba founded the city of Murcia (Mursiya) in 825.

4 El Cid (1043–99)
This charismatic knight won a considerable area of lands around Valencia from the Arabs.

5 Jaime I (1208–76)
The first Spanish king to make major gains against the Arabs in the Costa Blanca.

6 Isabella I (1451–1504) and Ferdinand V (1452–1516)
The Catholic monarchs held court at Orihuela in 1488, with the city at its most influential.

7 Rodrigo de Borja (1432–1503)
The infamous Pope Alexander VI, who fathered 10 children including Cesare and Lucrezia Borja, was born in Xàtiva (Játiva), Valencia.

8 Barbarroja (1475–1546)
Turkish pirate Jayr al-Din, better known as Barbarroja ("Red Beard"), was the scourge of the Mediterranean.

9 José de Ribera (1591–1652)
One of Spain's finest painters, he was born in Xàtiva, but spent most of his life in Italy.

10 José Moñino y Redondo (1728–1808)
A key figure in the Spanish Enlightenment, this reformist chief minister was born in Murcia.

Ancient sculpture of the Dama de Elx

TOP **10** Museums

Attractive interior of the Museo de Bellas Artes, Alicante

1 MUBAG (Museo de Bellas Artes), Alicante (Alacant)

This beautifully restored 18th-century palace houses a wide-ranging collection of paintings, sculpture, furniture, ceramics and engravings by Alicantino artists, with exhibits dating from the 16th century to the 20th century. Classical music concerts are frequently held in the museum during the evenings; check www.mubag.com for details *(see p17)*.

2 Museo Arqueológico, Villena

MAP C4 ■ Palacio Municipal, Plaza de Santiago 1 ■ 965 80 11 50 ■ Open 10am–2pm Tue–Sun ■ www.museovillena.com

The prize exhibit here is the Tesoro de Villena (Villena Treasure) – a Bronze Age hoard of bracelets, bowls, torcs and bottles, fashioned from thin sheets of beaten gold.

3 Museo del Calzado, Elda

MAP D4 ■ Avda de Chapí 32 ■ 965 38 30 21 ■ Open Sep–Jul: 10am–2pm & 5–8pm Tue–Sat, 10am–2pm Sun; Aug: 11am–2pm Tue–Fri ■ Adm ■ www.museocalzado.com

This museum in Spain's shoemaking capital documents the evolution of shoe design from the early spurred metal boots worn by medieval knights to the modern 21st-century creations.

4 Museo de Arte Contemporáneo, Alicante

MAP V2 ■ Plaza Santa Maria 3 ■ 965 21 31 56 ■ Open 10am–8pm Tue–Sat (from 11am in summer), 10am–2pm Sun & public hols ■ www.maca-alicante.es

This 17th-century building houses a collection donated by Eusebio Sempere, one of the finest Spanish artists of the 20th century. His paintings and sculptures, along with a large number of artworks from the 1950s, 1960s and 1970s, form the core of the museum's displays.

5 Museo San Juan de Dios, Orihuela

MAP P2 ▪ C/Hospital ▪ 686 75 40 27 ▪ Open 10am–2pm & 5–8pm Tue–Sat, 10am–2pm Sun

The 18th-century Hospital of San Juan de Dios is the home of Orihuela's archaeological museum, which tells the city's history from its beginnings to the 18th century. The eeriest exhibit is a 17th-century float depicting a she-devil known as *La Diablesa*.

6 Museo del Teatro Romano, Cartagena

MAP P5 ▪ C/Cuesta de la Baronesa ▪ 968 50 48 02 ▪ Open 10am–6pm Tue–Sat (May–Sep: to 8pm), 10am–2pm Sun ▪ Adm ▪ www.teatroromano.cartagena.es

Found in 1988 and beautifully restored, the Roman amphitheatre in Cartagena dates back to the 1st century BC. The museum is also home to a vast collection of archaeological remains.

7 MAHE, Elx (Elche)

MAP D6 ▪ Palau d'Altamira, Carrer Nou del Palau ▪ 966 65 82 03 ▪ Open 10am–6pm Mon–Sat, 10am–3pm Sun ▪ Adm

Situated in the Palacio de Altamira, this interactive museum displays a fine range of archaeological remains, which explain the history of Elx from its origins to the present day.

Visiting the MARQ museum, Alicante

8 MARQ, Alicante

This slickly designed museum brings Alicante's past to life. Don't miss the fascinating recreations of archaeological sites, including a shipwreck containing amphorae *(see p16)*.

9 Museo Salzillo, Murcia

MAP S5 ▪ Plaza San Agustín 3 ▪ 968 29 18 93 ▪ Open Jul & Aug: 10am–2pm Mon–Fri; Sep–Mar: 10am–5pm Mon–Sat, 11am–2pm Sun ▪ www.museosalzillo.es

Dedicated to the 18th-century Murcian sculptor Francisco Salzillo, this museum features a collection of gilded processional floats bearing his exquisite, emotional depictions of the Passion of Christ.

Painted figure, Museo Salzillo

10 Museo de l'Almudí, Xàtiva (Játiva)

MAP E1 ▪ C/Corretgeria 46 ▪ 962 27 65 97 ▪ Open mid-Jun–mid-Sep: 9:30am–2:30pm Tue–Fri, 10am–2:30pm Sat & Sun; mid-Sep–mid-Jun: 10am–2pm & 4–6pm Tue–Fri, 10am–2pm Sat & Sun ▪ Adm

This restored 16th-century granary houses an archaeology museum. Exhibits include fragments of Iberian sculpture and Visigothic capitals, as well as a collection of Roman inscriptions, the preserved arches of the town's ancient Arab baths and an 11th-century Islamic water trough.

Skeletal remains, MAHE, Elx

Churches and Cathedrals

1 Santa Iglesia Catedral del Salvador y Santa María, Orihuela

MAP P2 ▪ Plaza del Salvador ▪ 965 30 06 38 ▪ Open 10:30am–2pm & 4–6:30pm Mon–Fri, 10:30am–2pm & during Mass Sat & Sun

Orihuela's Gothic cathedral of pale, creamy stone was begun in the 14th century. There is exquisite sculptural detail inside and out. Two splendid wrought-iron grills enclose the choir, with its beautiful Baroque organ, and the cathedral's main altar.

Façade detail, Basílica de Santa María, Alicante

2 Ex-Colegiata de San Patricio, Lorca

MAP K4 ▪ Plaza España ▪ 968 46 99 66 ▪ Open 10:30am–1pm & 4:30–6pm daily

This grand church commemorates victories against the Arabs on the feast day of St Patrick in 1452. Begun in the mid-16th century, it was given a thorough Baroque overhaul in the 18th century.

3 Catedral de Santa María, Murcia

Murcia's impressive cathedral is best known for its flamboyant, sculpture-encrusted façade and elaborate bell tower *(see pp34–5)*.

4 Basílica de Santa María, Alicante (Alacant)

This delightful church was built on the ruins of Al-Lekant's main mosque. The soaring interior is pure Gothic, but the ornate Baroque façade was added in 1713 *(see p16)*.

5 Iglesia de San Bartolomé, Xàbia (Jávea)

MAP H3 ▪ Plaza de la Iglesia ▪ 965 79 11 74 ▪ Open 10:30am–12:30pm Mon–Fri

This fortress-church was begun in 1513, when the coastline was under constant attack from pirates, but the golden Tosca stone and its faded sculptural decoration make it truly charming.

6 Colegiata Basílica de Santa María, Xàtiva (Játiva)

MAP E1 ▪ Plaza Calixto III ▪ 962 28 14 81 (tourist office) ▪ Open 10:30am–1pm daily (from 11:30am Sun & public hols)

The grandest church in this "City of Popes" was begun in 1596, but is still unfinished. The façade was finally constructed in 1916; the second bell tower (proposed 300 years ago) has yet to be built.

Basílica de Santa María, Xàtiva

7 Basílica de Santa María, Elx (Elche)

MAP D6 ■ Plaza de Santa María ■ 965 45 15 40 ■ Open 7:30am–12:30pm & 6–8:30pm daily; Tower: summer: 11am–7pm daily, winter: 10:30am–3pm daily ■ Adm for the tower

Celebrated for its performances of the Misteri d'Elx *(see p75)*, the Basílica de Santa María was built between 1672 and 1783, replacing an earlier church built on the ruins of a former mosque.

8 Colegio de Santo Domingo, Orihuela

MAP P2 ■ C/Adolfo Claravana 63 ■ 965 30 02 40 ■ Open 9:30am–1:30pm & 4–7pm Tue–Sat (summer: 10am–2pm, 5–8pm), 10am–2pm Sun

Often dubbed the "El Escorial of the East" after the celebrated royal palace near Madrid, this enormous complex was built between the 16th and 18th centuries.

Colegio de Santo Domingo, Orihuela

9 Concatedral de San Nicolás de Bari, Alicante

Dedicated to the city's patron saint, Alicante's vast cathedral *(see p16)* was built in the sober Herrerian Renaissance style. Its most striking feature is the graceful blue cupola almost 50 m (164 ft) high.

10 Iglesia de San Martín, Callosa de Segura

MAP P2 ■ Plaza de la Iglesia ■ 966 75 70 59 ■ Open 10am–1pm & 8:30–9:30pm Tue, 10am–1pm Wed & Fri

Once one of the most affluent cities of the old Kingdom of Valencia, Callosa de Segura possesses one of the finest Renaissance churches in Spain.

Medieval Towns and Villages

1 Mula
Steeply mounted on a sheer cliff, pretty Mula *(see p110)* is known for the *Noche de los Tambores* (Night of the Drums), which takes place on Tuesday night of Holy Week *(see p114)*. Villagers and visitors can compete in *pánganas* or drum-offs.

Guadalest, a clifftop village

2 Guadalest
The most famous inland village in the Costa Blanca, Guadalest has a stunning setting atop a jagged crest in a sea of mountains *(see pp18–19)*.

3 Agres
MAP E3

This delightful mountain village topped by a ruined castle makes the perfect starting point for exploring the gorgeous Sierra de Mariola, with hiking trails and the traces of abandoned snow wells.

4 Cehegín
MAP K2

This pretty town perches gracefully on a hillside overlooking the river. Its elegant old quarter, with a swathe of medieval churches and mansions, still displays vestiges of its aristocratic past. The best views of the surrounding country are from a balustraded viewing point at the top.

5 Cocentaina
MAP E3

The ancient core of Cocentaina is a charming tangle of crooked streets set around the imposing Palau Condal. The palace marks the dividing point between the Christian and Arab quarters, which were established after the Reconquest. A ruined Arabic watchtower still stands guard on a lofty cliff.

6 Moratalla
Sleepy Moratalla lies on a steep hillside in the remotest corner of Murcia, a jumble of tiled rooftops under a castle built by the Arabs and then rebuilt after the Reconquest. A viewing point near the castle offers fine views *(see p111)*.

7 Bocairent
MAP D3

Unexpected steps and tiny passages link the steep streets of Bocairent, piled up on a hill in the Sierra de Mariola. Almost every house is

Medieval town of Bocairent

surrounded by pots of ferns and geraniums. In 1843, an extraordinary bullring was hacked out of the rock. It now regularly hosts summer concerts and bullfights.

Mountain village of Polop

Polop
MAP G4

Just a few miles inland from the hectic coast, Polop is a peaceful little village set on a hill surrounded by orchards. Polop's old quarter, with its maze of narrow streets recalling its Arabic origins, invites a tranquil stroll.

Caravaca de la Cruz

Beautifully set amid rolling hills, this medieval town once belonged to the Knights Templar, and it is still dominated by their 15th-century castle. Situated within the castle complex is the Santuario de la Vera Cruz *(see p109)*.

Penàguila
MAP F3

Time seems to have stood still in Penàguila, a small, picturesque village of ochre houses huddled around a sturdy 16th-century church. On the outskirts are the immaculate flower gardens and ponds of the 19th-century Jardín de Santos. Surrounded by magnificent mountains, the ruins of an ancient castle are set among forests high above the village.

TOP 10 CASTLES

1 Águilas
MAP L6
Beautifully floodlit at night, this lovely castle is perched right on the edge of a steep cliff *(see p103)*.

2 Villena
High above the town, this fairy-tale castle has towers and ramparts *(see p80)*.

3 Petrer (Petrel)
Precipitously balanced on a cliff, this castle was built by the Arabs *(see p91)*.

4 Xàtiva (Játiva)
The Romans built a fortress here, but the current castle dates back to the medieval period *(see p81)*.

5 Banyeres de Mariola
MAP D3
The highest of all the castles in the region, Banyeres de Mariola dominates from a towering peak.

6 Guadalest
Little is left of Guadalest's castle, but the ruins offer some fabulous panoramic views *(see pp18–19)*.

7 Castillo de Santa Bárbara, Alicante (Alacant)
This 16th-century fortress replaced the original Arabic castle *(see pp14–15)*.

8 La Mola
This curious castle features the only triangular tower in Europe *(see p93)*.

9 Dénia (Denia)
The design of Dénia's castle *(see p80)*, built on a rocky hilltop, dates back to the Muslim period *(see p38)*.

10 Biar
MAP D4
This well-preserved Arabic castle withstood a lengthy siege before finally falling to Jaime I *(see pp38–9)* in 1245

Arabic castle at Biar

🔟 Modernista Gems

② Casa Monerris Planelles, Xixona (Jijona)

MAP E4 ■ Avda de la Constitución 33–35–37 ■ Closed to public

The town of Xixona is most famous for its production of sweet *turrón* (nougat), but it also contains some handsome turn-of-the-20th-century buildings. This mansion, belonging to a family of *turroneros*, sports a lovely façade, with a charming turret covered with blue and gold tiles.

③ Casino, Torrevieja

MAP Q3 ■ Paseo Vistalegre 14 ■ 965 71 01 04 ■ Open 9am–11pm daily

Built at the end of the 19th century, Torrevieja's celebrated seafront casino is one of the purest examples of Modernista architecture in the region. The highlight is the Mozarabic salon, with a fabulous carved wooden ceiling, horseshoe arches and mosaic tiling.

① Real Casino, Murcia

MAP U5 ■ C/Trapería 18 ■ 968 21 53 99 ■ Open 10:30am–7pm daily ■ Adm (includes audioguide) ■ www. realcasinomurcia.com

This casino is a monument to eclecticism. Each room has its own theme, from the Arabic-style entrance hall to the flamboyant Rococo frills and flounces in the ballroom. And there's a special bonus for female visitors: the ceiling mural of primping nymphs in the ladies' restroom.

④ Palacio de Aguirre, Cartagena

MAP P5 ■ Plaza de la Merced 16 ■ 968 50 16 07 ■ Open 10am–2pm & 5–7pm Tue–Fri, 11am–2pm & 5–8pm Sat, 11am–2pm Sun & public hols

The most prolific Modernista architect in Cartagena at the turn of the 20th century, Victor Beltrí was responsible for this handsome mansion in the old town. It is decorated with shimmering mosaics and topped with a brilliant cupola, and its corner position ensures plenty of natural light. It now houses the city's Museum of Modern Art.

⑤ Casino, Cartagena

MAP P5 ■ C/Mayor 15 ■ 988 12 44 65 ■ Check website for opening hours ■ www.casinodecartagena.org

This 18th-century Baroque palace was completely overhauled at the end of the 19th century, when the Casino Círculo Cartagenero (a social and cultural club) took it over. Victor Beltrí was responsible for adding the ornate Modernista woodwork, floral tiling and exuberant plasterwork, which are now sadly neglected.

Ceiling mural at the Real Casino, Murcia

Stained-glass ceiling in the Casa-Museo Modernista, Novelda

⑥ Casa-Museo Modernista, Novelda

The most sumptuous Modernista mansion in the Costa Blanca has been exquisitely restored, and still contains much of its original furniture *(see pp22–3)*.

⑦ Gran Hotel, Cartagena

MAP P5 ■ C/Jara s/n ■ Info can be obtained from the Cartagena tourist office: 968 50 64 83 ■ Closed to public

Crowned with its trademark golden cupola, the most emblematic Modernista building in the whole of Cartagena, the opulent Gran Hotel, was begun in 1907 by Tomás Rico and completed by the indefatigable Victor Beltrí. Every window and archway is surrounded with swooping stone garlands. No longer a hotel, it now houses private offices, so visitors can just admire its exterior.

Gran Hotel, Cartagena

⑧ Casa Modernista, Jumilla

MAP A4 ■ C/Cánovas del Castillo 55 ■ Closed to public

This architectural gem of the early 20th century is tucked away in the quiet wine-producing town of Jumilla. Designed by a follower of Antoni Gaudí, it has impressive, highly ornate ironwork by local craftsman Avelino Gómez.

⑨ Círculo Industrial, Alcoi (Alcoy)

MAP E3 ■ C/Sant Nicolau 19 ■ 965 54 06 66 ■ Open 9am–9pm daily ■ www.circuloindustrial.es

Alcoi, still a busy industrial town, has several Modernista buildings. The Círculo Industrial (1868) was one of the earliest. Particularly worthy of note are the flowing ironwork and ceramic details in its fine salons and library. Designed as a cultural centre, it still hosts art exhibitions and the occasional concert. It also has a restaurant.

⑩ Casa de El Piñón, La Unión

MAP P5 ■ C/Mayor s/n ■ Info can be obtained from La Unión tourist office: 968 541 614 ■ Open 9am–2pm Mon–Fri ■ Closed public hols

The Casa de El Piñón is one of the best examples of Murcian eclecticism, bristling with florid decoration and topped with a cupola, which was designed by Gustave Eiffel, of Eiffel Tower fame. The building was restored after years of neglect, and now houses the local city hall.

⭐10 Resorts

Buildings lining the picturesque seafront at Xàbia

1 Benidorm

The biggest and best known of the Costa Blanca resorts, Benidorm is a mini-Manhattan of skyscrapers set around an impressive bay. Its immaculate beaches, two sweeping curves of soft golden sand, are the finest in the region, and the wide choice of restaurants and nightlife is second to none (see p80).

2 Dénia (Denia)

Now a relaxed family resort with superb beaches and a busy port, Dénia had a long and glorious history before tourism hit the Mediterranean coast – first as a Roman settlement, then as the capital of an Arabic kingdom. For respite from the summer crowds, take a hike in the nearby Montgó Natural Park (see p80).

Castle overlooking Dénia harbour

3 Xàbia (Jávea)

The pretty tumble of old Xàbia sits on a hilltop a couple of miles inland from the sea. The bay forms a horseshoe, with both pebbly and sandy beaches, and a spectacular cape at both ends (see p79).

4 Puerto de Mazarrón

This sprawling family resort has several sandy beaches spread on either side of a rocky headland, which has an attractive coastal path. The inland village of Mazarrón is a lovely tranquil spot – perfect for a break from the beach (see p102).

5 Calp (Calpe)
MAP G3

Calp has a stunning natural setting on a vast bay dominated by the Penyal d'Ifac (see pp20–21). The modern resort has almost swallowed up the original medieval village, but its sandy beaches and excellent watersports facilities have made it immensely popular.

6 Altea
MAP G4

Pretty Altea, piled on a hill overlooking the sea and topped with a blue-domed church, has long attracted artists, and the old quarter has many arty shops and galleries. A narrow, pebbly beach is backed by a seafront promenade.

7 Torrevieja

Torrevieja is a low-key family resort with some great sandy beaches and an unusual but attractive seafront, with rock pools accessed by ladders. The salt lagoons that lie on the outskirts of town have been designated a Natural Park *(see p91)*.

8 La Vila Joiosa (Villajoyosa)

The Jewelled Town gets its name from the brightly painted houses clustered around the port. It has fine sandy beaches, a smattering of historic buildings, and a centuries-old chocolate-making tradition, which is recounted in the town's chocolate museum *(see p67)*.

Colourful houses in La Vila Joiosa

9 La Manga de Mar Menor

On this extraordinary built-up strip of sand *(see p102)* you have the choice of two seas: the sheltered lagoon of the Mar Menor, which is a great place to learn to sail, and the Mediterranean. The resort has excellent facilities for many activities, in and out of the water.

10 Águilas

Águilas is beautifully set on a curving bay against a backdrop of distant mountains. It has some handsome 19th-century squares, a castle high on a cliff above the fishing port, and secluded coves on the outskirts *(see p103)*.

TOP 10 QUIET RESORTS

Dehesa de Campoamor beach

1 Dehesa de Campoamor
This modern resort of low-rise villas and apartments is set around long, golden sands.

2 Moraira-Teulada
A smart enclave of whitewashed villas on a rugged coastline, Moraira-Teulada has quiet coves and a marina.

3 El Campello
Despite the proximity of the busy beaches at San Juan, this fishing village retains its tranquil atmosphere.

4 Guardamar del Segura
This is a small family resort that is blessed with wonderful, wild dune-backed beaches.

5 Oliva
Escape the crowds in this peaceful village, just 4 km (2 miles) away from lengthy golden beaches.

6 Lo Pagán
The smallest resort on the Mar Menor, Lo Pagán has some great seafood restaurants on the beach.

7 Portús
This tiny village overlooks a narrow, sandy beach with colourful fishing boats. Its relative seclusion makes it popular with naturists.

8 Bolnuevo
On the fringes of Puerto de Mazarrón, Bolnuevo has long sandy beaches and hidden coves to the south.

9 La Azohía
On the unspoiled cape of Tiñoso, this fishing village is one of the quietest resorts in the region.

10 Calabardina
A charming little resort tucked under a dramatic headland and overlooking a delightful bay.

Beaches

1 Playa Nord, Gandia-Playa

MAP F1

This immaculate golden beach is famously "combed" by tractors in summer to keep it pristine. Lined with smart rows of sunshades and blue-and-white-striped sun loungers, it has all the amenities, plus a line of restaurants and cafés along the front.

2 Les Aigües Blanques, Oliva

MAP G2

Oliva is blessed with long, sandy beaches that extend for miles, so there's always a quiet spot if you are prepared to walk. This beach, with its extensive dunes, is the largest and best equipped, with every amenity.

3 Les Rotes, Dénia (Denia)

MAP H2

This is a delightful pebbly stretch of rock pools, tiny islands and hidden coves, where you can usually find a quiet corner. It has good amenities and a breezy seafront promenade lined with restaurants and cafés.

4 Playa de Bolnuevo, Bolnuevo

MAP M5

The main beach of this sleepy little resort is long and sandy, with good facilities including lifeguards, cafés and restaurants. Behind it are the extraordinary cliffs of the "enchanted city" *(see p102)*. To the south, naturists will find a series of secluded coves.

Playa de Levante, Benidorm

5 Playa de Levante, Benidorm

MAP H6

Benidorm's south-facing Playa de Levante is one of the most famous beaches in Europe – a long golden arc of sand stretching from the old town to the foot of the Sierra Helada. It has various facilities including playgrounds, ecological toilet cubicles and even a beach library.

6 Calblanque

With golden beaches, secluded coves, cliff walks and forested hills, Calblanque is one of the most beautiful stretches of the Costa Blanca. It has very few facilities, so bring picnic things and plenty to drink. Take care in the water: the current can be dangerous *(see pp12–13)*.

Picturesque Playa de Bolnuevo

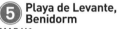

7 Dunas de Guardamar, Guardamar del Segura

These gorgeous, windswept dunes are rarely crowded, even in the height of summer. They are part of a natural reserve backed by a pine forest with walking trails, interesting archaeological remains and picnic spots. There are a few snack bars here, but not much else *(see p90)*.

8 Portitxol, Cap de la Nau (Cabo de la Nao)
MAP H3

Flanked by high cliffs and looking out over the tiny island of Portitxol, this is another exquisite cove. The *mirador* (viewing point) above the cove offers some of the most beautiful views on the whole coastline. Local amenities include café-bars and a lifeguard post.

9 Playa de San Juan, Alicante (Alacant)
MAP E5

Easily the best of Alicante's beaches, this glorious stretch of fine sand with every facility is in a popular holiday suburb a short tram ride from the city centre. The bars and clubs buzz all night in summer.

10 La Granadella, Cap de la Nau
MAP H3

The only way in and out of this tiny, pebbly cove is down a narrow road that twists and turns its way to the perfect curve of the bay. The blue-green water is overlooked by cliffs, and the small rocky beach is backed by a handful of beach bars and restaurants.

TOP 10 BEACH TIPS

Lifeguard beach hut

1 Lifeguards
Most beaches, even more remote ones, will have a lifeguard post in summer.

2 Warning Flags
Don't swim if a red, black or no flag is flying, and be cautious if you see a yellow flag. A green flag means it is safe to swim.

3 Facilities
Town beaches generally offer excellent facilities, including play areas, foot showers and refreshments.

4 Jellyfish
Jellyfish can be a nuisance. If you get stung, larger beaches will have a *Cruz Roja* (Red Cross) medical post.

5 Blue Flags
Blue Flags are awarded to beaches that have achieved a high standard of cleanliness and offer good facilities.

6 Sunscreen
Don't forget your sunscreen. The sun is very fierce on the Costa Blanca. You should avoid sunbathing between the hours of noon and 4pm.

7 Water
Ensure you bring an adequate water supply with you, particularly when staying on remote beaches.

8 Beach bars
Many beaches have snack bars, or *xiringuitos*, which are open only during the summer months.

9 Beating the crowds
The Costa Blanca is highly developed, and city beaches are always crammed, but you can always find a quiet corner.

10 Wheelchair Access
Many beaches, particularly those in the cities, have ramps for wheelchair access. The tourist office will have details.

🔟 Wine Towns

The pretty hillside town of Jumilla

① Jumilla

One of the largest Murcian wine-producing towns, Jumilla spills down a hillside, overlooked by a 15th-century castle *(see p110)*. The town has been producing wine since Roman times. The local *bodegas* make a robust red from Monastrell and a rosé from Garnacha grapes.

② Alguenya (Algueña)
MAP C5

This small agricultural village is well known for its hearty traditional cuisine, particularly cured sausages. The local wine, a strong, earthy red produced under the D.O. of Alicante, is perfect with regional dishes.

③ Xaló (Jalón)
MAP G3

Dominated by its striking 19th-century church, the formerly sleepy village of Xaló is now surrounded by villas and holiday-home developments. Tourism

Vineyards near the village of Xaló

is now its biggest source of income, but some traditions, including wine-production, have continued. There are several *bodegas*, with reds, whites, rosés and a sweet white *mistela* wine.

④ El Pinós (Pinoso)
MAP C5

Sitting peacefully on a low hill in a broad, vine-covered plain, El Pinós is an affluent little town with a rambling old centre curling around a pretty clock tower. It made its fortune from salt and cured sausages, but it is also an important wine-producing town. Try the vigorous young reds at one of many *bodegas*.

⑤ Abanilla
MAP N1

Abanilla is a small agricultural town known for its palm groves. It sits just inside Murcia province, but produces much of its wine under the Alicante D.O. The robust reds and whites are usually drunk young and are ideally suited to the earthy local cuisine.

⑥ Monóvar

A cheerful old town dotted with historic monuments, Monóvar is one of the biggest wine-producing towns in the Alicante region. At the many *bodegas* you can pick up some potent local red, a fresh rosé or the celebrated El Fondillón, a sweet dessert wine that takes a minimum of 10 years to mature *(see p92)*.

7 Hondón
MAP C5

Blink and you'll miss these two tiny hamlets in the middle of a vast plain with vines stretching in every direction. Hondón de las Nieves and Hondón de los Frailes are just off the Monóvar–Jumilla road. Their table wines are available from the large *bodegas* which line the road.

8 Bullas
MAP L2

This medieval village, still guarded by the remnants of a castle, sits in a valley with endless rows of vines. Wine has been produced here since Roman times; you can learn about its history at the local Museo del Vino. The area is good for rosés and red table wines.

Vines and almond blossom, Teulada

9 Teulada
MAP H3

The upmarket resort of Teulada has long been famous for its moscatel grapes, grown along the sunny hillsides and sold in markets and at roadside stalls. They are used to make its delicious and refreshing sweet white *mistela* wine, which you will find at countless local *bodegas*.

10 Yecla
MAP B4

Yecla is the prettiest wine town in the Costa Blanca, with a smattering of historic churches and buildings. It's best known for its red wines, which are generally light and fruity. Many *bodegas* offer tastings and tours.

TOP 10 BODEGAS

Casks in a *bodega*

1 Bodegas Balcona
MAP K2 ▪ Ctra Avilés Km 10, Paraje de Aceniche, Bullas ▪ 968 65 28 91
Try this bodega's Partal Crianza.

2 Bodegas Carchelo
MAP A4 ▪ Casa de la Hoya s/n, Paraje El Carche, Jumilla ▪ 968 43 51 37
Excellent reds are produced here.

3 Bodegas Bleda
MAP A4 ▪ Ctra de Ontur, Km 2, Jumilla ▪ 968 78 00 12
Try the award-winning Divus.

4 Bodegas Gutiérrez de la Vega
MAP G3 ▪ C/Les Quintanes 1, Parcent ▪ 966 40 38 71
Be sure to try the justly celebrated 2012 Imagine Tinto.

5 Bodegas E Mendoza
MAP G4 ▪ Partida El Romeral s/n, L'Alfas del Pì ▪ 965 88 86 39
Taste the excellent Reserva Santa Rosa.

6 Bodegas Castaño
MAP B4 ▪ Ctra Fuenteálamo 3, Yecla ▪ 968 79 11 15
Very reputable, with good, fruity reds.

7 Bodegas Monóvar
MAP D5 ▪ Ctra Monóvar Salinas, Km 3.2, Monóvar ▪ 965 92 88 57
Try some of the famous Fondillón wine.

8 Bodegas Heretat de Cesilia
MAP D5 ▪ Paraje Alcaydías 4, Novelda ▪ 965 60 37 63
Pay a visit to enjoy the fine wines and views of the vineyards.

9 Bodega de Pinoso
MAP C5 ▪ Paseo de la Constitución 82, Pinoso ▪ 965 47 70 40
Award-winning organic wines.

10 Bodegas Francisco Gómez
MAP C3 ▪ Ctra Villena – Pinoso Km 8.8, Villena ▪ 965 97 95 55
Taste the local Monastrell wines.

🔟 Areas of Natural Beauty

1 Fonts d'Algar

These enchanting waterfalls, tucked away in an orchard-lined valley, spill down the hillside and form a series of delightful natural swimming pools. A wooden staircase eases the ascent to the highest pool, which is shaded by willow trees and makes a perfect picnic spot *(see p57)*.

Natural pool at the Fonts d'Algar

2 Parc Natural del Carrascal de la Font Roja
MAP E3

One of the few surviving stretches of indigenous Mediterranean oak forest, this glorious expanse of woodland is a cool, shady Natural Park scattered with ancient snow wells (used to collect ice in the days before refrigeration) and crisscrossed with pretty walking trails offering spectacular views of endless mountains.

3 Parc Natural del Montgó
MAP H2

The pale massif of Montgó looms high above the seaside resorts of Dénia (Denia) and Xàbia (Jávea). Delightful walking trails meander through flower-strewn scrub and woodland, past ancient caves and up to stunning viewpoints that gaze out across the sierra and over the sea.

4 Isla de Benidorm
MAP G4

The natural beauty of this curious, triangular island in the middle of Benidorm Bay is best appreciated underwater, for the Isla de Benidorm is a marine reserve and home to a wonderful array of sea life, from sea anemones to octopus, stingray and scorpion fish.

5 Isla Tabarca

Tabarca, the only inhabited island on the Costa Blanca, has beautiful pebbly coves, a sandy bay, and a charming old town complete with a winsome little church right on the water's edge *(see pp30–31)*.

6 Ciudad Encantada de Bolnuevo

The pale sandstone cliffs behind Bolnuevo Beach have been shaped over time into an extraordinary "enchanted city"; it doesn't take much to see towers and castles in the creamy swirls of rock, some of which are poised on impossibly thin pedestals *(see p102)*.

Sandstone cliffs of the Ciudad Encantada

7 Penyal d'Ifac (Peñón de Ifach)

A vast, sheer rock erupting from the turquoise sea, the Penyal d'Ifac is now a natural park with a magnificent walking trail that leads you right to the summit *(see pp20–21)*.

8 Cap de la Nau (Cabo de la Nao)

The epitome of the Costa Blanca, this rugged cape with tiny, magical coves and sheer cliffs offers superb views along the coastline. While parts are covered with villas, there are still some beautiful undisturbed corners to explore *(see p83)*.

Stunning view of the Cap de la Nau

9 Sierra Espuña

This magnificent range of pine-clad mountains is one of the few green corners of arid Murcia. Walking trails offer glimpses of forested slopes and rocky outcrops, and birds of prey circle lazily, high above the treetops *(see pp26–7)*.

10 Calblanque

Calblanque Regional Park is one of Murcia's best-kept secrets. Just a few minutes' drive from the resorts of the Mar Menor, this stretch of unspoiled coastline has hidden coves and gorgeous sandy beaches with clear waters *(see pp12–13)*.

TOP 10 TREES, PLANTS AND WILDLIFE

Orange trees laden with fruit

1 Fruit Trees
The orchards of the Costa Blanca produce an abundance of almonds, citrus fruit and cherries.

2 Spanish Broom
This hardy evergreen is a beautiful sight in spring, when its glorious yellow blooms carpet the countryside.

3 Valencian Rock Violet
This pretty, purple, cliff-dwelling flower thrives in damp, salty conditions.

4 Holm Oak
With its dark, waxy leaves, this evergreen is very common across the Iberian Peninsula.

5 Wild Herbs
Rosemary, thyme and lavender scent the scrubby slopes, particularly around Montgó Natural Park.

6 Gulls
Many species of gull breed along the Costa Blanca, including the endangered Audouin's gull, with its trademark red bill and dark feet.

7 Birds of Prey
Eagles, hawks and vultures swoop silently above the more remote sierras of the northern Costa Blanca.

8 Flamingos
During the summer, flamingos come to breed on the salt lakes at Santa Pola, Torrevieja and the Mar Menor.

9 Ibex
This nimble mountain goat once faced extinction, but is now flourishing in the sierras of the northern Costa Blanca and parts of Murcia.

10 Wild Boar
These tusked, shaggy-coated mammals are common in most of the forested inland regions of the Costa Blanca.

🔟 Drives

Almond trees in full blossom covering the Xaló valley

1 Coll de Rates and Xaló Valley
MAP G3

From Benidorm or Altea, go up to Callosa d'en Sarrià (see p81) then take the winding road up through Tàrbena to the Coll de Rates pass. The route then drops down through Parcent into the bucolic Xaló (Jalón) Valley, where there are restaurants for lunch. Meet the coast road at Benissa to get back to the start.

2 Around the Sierra Espuña
MAP L3–M3

The twisting road through this mountainous nature reserve begins near Aledo. Make a detour to Collado Bermejo to see the snow wells (see p26), and then follow the right fork in

Verdant view of the Sierra Espuña

the road for a lunch stop and to visit the tourist information office. Continue on the same road to Alhama de Murcia before returning to Aledo.

3 Vall de Gallinera
MAP G2–F3

If you can, visit the Vall de Gallinera in spring, when the scent of almond blossom fills the air, and the hillsides are covered in a sea of pink and white. Follow the Ruta dels 8 Pobles, a scenic 14-km (9-mile) drive that links eight enchanting villages between Benirrama and Benissili. Local tourist offices can provide a map.

4 Simat de Valldigna from Gandia (Gandía)
MAP F2–F1

A pleasant drive takes you northwest from Gandia, first to the coastal viewpoint of Mondúber (near La Drova), and then to the restored Royal Cistercian monastery, Monestir de Santa Maria de la Valldigna, at Simat de Valldigna (the name means "the valley fit for a king"). The road beyond links up with the main coastal road to get back to Gandia.

5 Sierra de Mariola
MAP E3–D3

Alcoi (Alcoy) is the departure point for a tour of the austere but beautiful mountains of the Sierra de Mariola, stopping at Cocentaina *(see p44)*, a medieval town; Agres *(see p44)*, the departure point for a great walk; and Bocairent *(see pp44–5)*, a charming hilltop town. Complete your journey with a drive back to Alcoi.

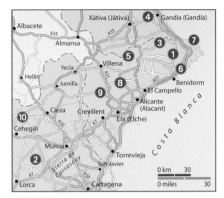

6 Vall de Guadalest
MAP E3–G4

From the seaside resort of Altea to the hilltop village of Penàguila, this drive takes in waterfalls and natural pools of the Fonts d'Algar near Callosa d'en Sarrià *(see p81)*, the precipitous village of Guadalest overlooking a turquoise reservoir *(see pp18–19)*, and the serene, castle-topped village of Penàguila.

Reservoir at Guadalest

7 Coast Road, Dénia (Denia) to La Granadella
MAP H2–3

This coastal drive twists over hills past the Natural Park of Montgó, through pretty Xàbia (Jávea), around the dramatic Cap de la Nau (Cabo de la Nao) headland, to tiny La Granadella cove. One to avoid in high summer.

8 Maigmó and Tibi
MAP E4

A half-day trip northwest from Alicante (Alacant) leads to the Sierra de Maigmó, clad in pinewoods. Part of this mountain range is a nature reserve, and there are footpaths to explore. At nearby Tibi, an ancient dam blends into the landscape *(see*

p93), a good place for a picnic. Combine this trip with shopping in Agost, famous for ceramics *(see p92)*.

9 Wine Country: Monóvar, Jumilla, Yecla
MAP A4–C5

Take a tour of the *bodegas* in the delightful wine towns of Monóvar, Jumilla and Yecla *(see pp52–3)*. Lost in a sea of vines, this drive is at its best in the late summer or early autumn just before harvest. Begin at sleepy Monóvar and finish in Yecla, the largest and prettiest of the three.

10 Vall del Segura
MAP N3–K1

This drive follows the Segura River from the cosmopolitan city of Murcia to the country town of Calasparra *(see p111)*. Along the way, visit Archena's pretty spa, then meander through the green Ricote valley up to historic Cieza, past the lake of Alfonso XIII, before arriving at the rice fields of Calasparra.

Hilltop village in the Vall de Segura

🔟 Outdoor Activities

1 Adventure Sports
The mountainous inland regions are superb for adventure sports. You can try your hand at canyon-descent, bungee-jumping, kayaking, rafting, paragliding, spelunking quad-biking or off-roading.

2 Fishing
This is an obsession in Spain, but be aware that permits are required for both freshwater and deep-sea fishing. Contact the tourist information offices for details. If you take an organized fishing holiday, however, the tour company will usually arrange these for you.

3 Cycling
Cycling is a very popular sport in Spain. Some resorts have bike-rental facilities if you simply want to cruise the region on two wheels, and the Natural Parks have several off-road trails for mountain-bikers. There are some great cycling routes in the Costa Blanca, including green ways – converted railway lines (see pp60–61).

4 Diving
The Costa Blanca offers endless possiblities for underwater exploration. Several areas have been declared marine reserves, including the Cap de Sant Antoni near Xàbia (Jávea), the Isla de Benidorm (see p54),

Diving near Benidorm

the Penyal d'Ifac (Peñon de Ifach) (see pp20–21) and the Isla Tabarca (see pp30–31). Companies offer diving courses and trips in all major resorts.

5 Snorkelling
Good spots to try are Les Rotes (see p50), La Granadella (see p51) and off Isla Tabarca (see pp30–31). Always dive with a trained instructor.

6 Hiking
The coastal cliffs and inland sierras of the region are perfect for climbing and hiking (see pp60–61). The Penyal d'Ifac (Peñon de Ifach) and the Sierra de Bernia have several challenging climbing routes, and the Regional Parks, particularly the Sierra Espuña (see pp26–7), Font Roja (see p54), Montgó (see p60) and Calblanque (see pp12–13), offer great hikes and walking trails.

Hiking in Alicante province

7 Golf

With year-round sunshine and mild temperatures, it's no surprise that the Costa Blanca is one of Europe's top golfing destinations. There are almost 30 courses, the best known being the deluxe La Manga Club (see p105).

8 Sailing and Other Watersports

Most resorts have a marina offering everything from sailing courses to yacht charter and skipper hire. The biggest marinas are in Benidorm, Calp (Calpe), Alicante (Alacant), Torrevieja and Santiago de la Ribera. Surfing, windsurfing, water-skiing and jet-skiing are also popular. You'll find facilities for these in the larger resorts.

Sailing off the Costa Blanca

9 Bird-Watching

The Costa Blanca region is a veritable paradise for bird-watching enthusiasts. The salt lagoons in Calp, Santa Pola, Torrevieja and Calblanque attract numerous aquatic birds, and the sierras, particularly the Regional Park of the Sierra Espuña, are home to eagles and other birds of prey.

10 Horse Riding

There are horse-riding centres across the region, and most can organize anything from pony rides for kids to cross-country hacks. Tourist information offices have useful lists of local riding centres.

TOP 10 GOLF COURSES

Villaitana golf course, Benidorm

1 Villaitana (Benidorm)
MAP F4 ▪ www.meliavillaitanagolf.com
The best of the four golf courses near Benidorm, Villaitana has 36 holes.

2 La Sella (Dénia)
MAP H3 ▪ www.lasellagolf.com
Three 9-hole courses located next to Montgó nature reserve.

3 Oliva Nova (south of Gandia)
MAP G2 ▪ www.olivanova.com
A popular pitch-and-putt course, plus an 18-hole course designed by golfer Severiano Ballesteros.

4 Bonalba (Muchamiel)
MAP E5 ▪ hotelbonalba.com
An 18-hole course, with a hotel on site, within easy reach of Alicante.

5 Alicante
MAP E5 ▪ alicantegolf.com
A Ballesteros-designed 18-hole course located behind the Playa de San Juan.

6 El Plantio (Alicante/Elx)
MAP D6 ▪ elplantio.com
A hotel and apartments are adjacent to this 18-hole course plus pitch and putt.

7 La Finca (Torrevieja)
MAP P2 ▪ golflafinca.com
This long 18-hole course has plenty of challenging water features.

8 Altorreal (Murcia)
MAP N2 ▪ golfaltorreal.es
This 18-hole course is hillier than others in the area, and is great value for money.

9 La Manga
MAP Q5 ▪ lamangaclub.com
The famous La Manga has three 18-hole courses plus pitch and putt.

10 Lorca golf resort
MAP K4 ▪ lorcaresort.com
An 18-hole course and part of a growing resort with a residential area attached.

TOP 10 Walks and Cycling Routes

1 Northeast Murcia Green Way (Cycle Route)
MAP N3–K2

By far the longest cycle track in the region covers 76.8 km (48 miles) from the city of Murcia (see p108) to Caravaca de la Cruz (see p109). It runs along an abandoned railway line, and some of the former stations are now guesthouses. The landscapes along the way are very varied: first, the fertile farmlands of the Segura valley, then the badlands around the Mula River and finally the pinewoods and almond groves of the hills of the Murcia interior.

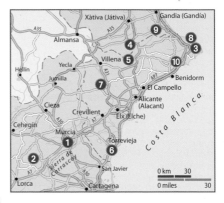

Hiking in the Sierra Espuña

2 Sierra Espuña (Walk)
MAP L3

The Sierra Espuña is probably the best place for walking in the area, with a range of trails adapted to hikers of all abilities. There are short trails for families, and more demanding hikes for advanced walkers (see pp26–7).

3 Peak of Montgó (Walk)

The hike to the top of Montgó begins at the entrance to Montgó Natural Park and climbs steadily, past ancient caves and scrubby hills

covered with wild herbs and flowers, up to La Creueta at 753 m (2,470 ft). The hike is easy, but takes about 3 hours each way so come prepared. It is well worth it, though, for the dramatic coastline views that unfold along the way (see p83).

4 Montcabrer (Walk)
MAP E3

An hour's climb from the village of Agres (see p44) into the Sierra de Mariola brings you to the picturesque ruins of two neveras (ice pits) that were built on the northern slopes of the mountains to help preserve food in the days before refrigerators. You can continue for a further half hour to the summit of Montcabrer, the highest summit in the range at 1,390 m (4,560 ft).

5 Parc Natural del Carrascal de la Font Roja (Walk)

The sanctuary at the heart of this nature reserve is a popular weekend day trip for locals (see p54). The shady walking paths through the cooler Mediterranean oak forest are the perfect respite from searing summer heat. There are several walking trails here and they suit hikers of all abilities, with the easiest (suitable for families) leaving from the sanctuary itself.

6 Las Salinas Green Way (Cycle Route)
MAP Q3

An easy pedal from Torrevieja is this there-and-back cycle track along the green way (former railway line) that runs for 6.7 km (4 miles) around the edge of a salt lagoon. It starts on Avenida de la Estación and finishes at a road in the outskirts of town. The first part is tarmac; after that you are cycling on compacted earth. At the end, return the same way you came.

7 The GR7 Long-Distance Footpath (Walk)

Gran Recorrido 7 connects Gibraltar with Andorra via Eastern Spain and ultimately extends to Greece. It goes through the inland mountains of Murcia and Alicante (Alacant), tracing a north-south route via Calasparra, Cieza, Pinoso, Elda, Castalla and Alcoi (Alcoy).

8 Dénia (Denia) (Cycle Route)
MAP H2

North of the resort there is a 6-km (4-mile) cycle track through orange groves along the route of the old narrow-gauge Carcaixent-Dénia railway. Along the way is a disused station, a level-crossing keeper's cottage and five rest areas. To start, take Avenida de Gandia and turn off left down Partida Negrals.

View over the coastal resort of Dénia

Gorge along the Racó del Duc

9 Racó del Duc (Walk)
MAP F2

An old railway line has been converted into an excellent walking path, which follows the River Serpis over bridges and through tunnels, past gorges, waterfalls and woodland glades, from Villalonga to L'Orxa. It's an easy trail and about 3–4 hours long. Bring a picnic and a swimming costume.

10 Sierra de Bernia (Walk)
MAP G3

There are several hikes from the Fonts d'Algar; a short walk from the falls will bring you to the ruins of the Fortress of Bernia, where seasoned walkers can carry on to the much tougher circuit around the peak itself.

TOP10 Children's Attractions

1 Cuevas de Canelobre

One of the biggest attractions on the Costa Blanca, this vast cavern is a short drive inland from Alicante (Alacant) *(see p90)*. Theatrically lit in bright colours, it is very impressive and is a great place to escape the midday heat in summer. It takes its name from an amazing limestone outcrop in the form of a candelabra.

Inside the Cuevas de Canelobre

2 Aquopolis, Torrevieja

MAP Q3 ■ Avda Delfina Viudes 99 ■ 965 71 58 90 ■ Check website for opening timings ■ Adm ■ www.torrevieja.aquopolis.es

This large water park is a lot of fun and has everything to keep the kids happy, from water slides of all heights and shapes to wave pools and assorted swimming pools. There are special areas for toddlers, and plenty of snack bars and ice-cream shops.

3 Dinopark

MAP F3 ■ Cactus d'Algar, Les Fonts d'Algar near Callosa d'en Sarria ■ 636 27 74 66 ■ Open Mar–Nov: daily ■ Closed Dec–Feb ■ Adm ■ www.dinopark.es

Robotic and static models of dinosaurs are scattered around this botanical garden, which includes a specimen of one of the world's oldest and rarest plants, the Wollemi pine. There is also a 3D cinema, lake, kids' playground and picnic area.

4 Terra Mítica

MAP F4 ■ Ctra Benidorm-Finestrat, Partida del Moralet s/n ■ 902 02 02 20 ■ Open Jul & Aug: daily; Jun & Sep: Tue–Sun; May & Oct: Thu–Sun; mid-Mar–Apr: Sat & Sun (precise hours vary, call or check online in advance) ■ Closed Nov–mid-Mar ■ Adm ■ www.terramiticapark.com

The biggest, most exciting theme park on the Costa Blanca, Terra Mítica has it all, from thrilling rollercoasters to huge water slides. Each section is dedicated to one of the great Mediterranean civilizations, including the Romans, Greeks, Egyptians and Iberians.

Riding the swing chairs at Terra Mítica park

Pool at Aqualandia, Benidorm

5 Aqualandia, Benidorm

MAP G4 ■ Sierra Helada, Rincon de Loix ■ 965 86 01 00 ■ Call ahead or check website for opening times ■ Adm ■ www.aqualandia.net

Europe's tallest slide and one of the world's highest capsule slides are among the 15 aquatic attractions in Spain's longest-running water park.

6 Aqua Natura, Murcia

MAP N2 ■ C/Regidor Cayetano Gago Espinardo, Murcia ■ 968 36 82 00 ■ Open 11am daily; closing time varies ■ Closed 1 Jan & 25 Dec ■ Adm ■ www.murcla. terranatura.com

Murcia's only water park is attached to Terra Natura wildlife park. It has pools, slides and tubes for slow or fast descent.

7 Mundo Marino

MAP H2, H3, G3, G4 ■ Various departure points ■ 966 42 30 66 ■ Times vary ■ Adm ■ www.mundomarino.es

A great way to admire the coastline is to take a ride in a glass-bottomed boat. This service offers full-day trips (including barbecues on board) from Dénia (Denia), Xàbia (Jávea), Calp (Calpe) and Altea.

8 Pola Park, Santa Pola

MAP E6, Q1 ■ Avda Zaragoza s/n ■ 965 41 70 60 ■ Open Jul & Aug: 7pm–1am daily; mid-Mar–Jun, Sep & Oct: check website ■ Closed Nov–mid-Mar ■ Adm ■ www.polapark.com

This fun park on the edge of Santa Pola has more than 20 attractions, including pirate boats and other rides.

9 Tentegorra Aventura

MAP N5 ■ Parque Rafael de la Cerda, Tentegorra, near Cartagena ■ 689 25 01 79 ■ Open Sat, Sun & public hols (by arrangement at other times for groups) ■ Adm ■ www. tentegorraventura.com

This complex within a park has three swimming pools with slides and a maze, as well as ladders, walkways and zipwires in the trees, creating a challenging adventure playground.

10 Karting Finestrat

MAP F4 ■ Ptda La Foia ampla, Finestrat s/n ■ 965 97 22 27 ■ Call ahead or check website for opening hours ■ Adm ■ www. kartingfinestrat.com

A popular daytime venue, with a 1-km- (0.6-mile-) long, 10-m- (11-yard-) wide track and a choice of high-powered vehicles for adults, while children have their own karts and a separate track.

🔟 Nightspots

Holidaymakers enjoying the bustling nightlife of Benidorm

1 C/Mallorca, C/Ibiza and C/Palma, Benidorm

MAP G4

Benidorm's nightlife is divided by nationality: these streets are the heart of the English section, and they are lined with a large number of popular British bars. Most offer live music, karaoke, theme nights, cabaret and other forms of entertainment.

2 Café Noray, Alicante (Alacant)

MAP U3 ▪ Paseo Conde de Vallellano s/n

Find a seat on Café Noray's lovely open-air terrace overlooking the marina, and enjoy the fine view of Alicante's seafront. This is a great place to have a coffee or a refreshing gin and tonic, wine or beer before heading out for the evening.

3 Frontera, Alicante

The musical programme at this well-established live rock bar near SanJuan beach might include anything from disco to funk, but the emphasis is firmly on traditional rock and blues. Thursday nights feature jam sessions for budding rock musicians and are enormously popular (see p96).

4 Penélope Beach Club, Benidorm

One of Benidorm's coolest clubs, with a perfect beachfront location, this is a great place to start the night. It has top DJs, dancers and a stylish crowd. The action starts late, when the music hots up and the go-gos get going (see p84).

5 Jokers, Benidorm

Excellent tribute acts such as Meatloaf (Albondigas) and the Rat Pack frequently perform at this popular, spacious bar-club. If dancing isn't your thing, you can relax with a cocktail on the terrace (see p84).

6 C Breeze Lounge Bar, Torrevieja

This friendly piano bar is family-run and offers a wide range of delicious, freshly made cocktails and a good selection of cava, wine and beer (see p96).

7 Magma Club, Alicante

MAP E5 ▪ Carrer Vial Flora de España ▪ 660 53 03 36 ▪ Closed Sun–Wed ▪ www.magmaclub.es

One of the most popular discos in Alicante, Magma Club hosts renowned DJs. There's also a restaurant and a garden.

8 Sala Musik, Murcia

MAP V5 ■ Plaza De Toros De Murcia Paseo de Garay 14 ■ 605 85 70 75 ■ www.iboleleproducciones.com/sala-musik

Located on the ground floor, this is one of Murcia's best live music venues. Each room hosts different types of music events, like intimate gigs and lively concerts. The varied programmes on offer span every music style from indie to pop to flamenco.

9 Zona de Las Tascas, Murcia

MAP U5

Murcia has a vibrant social scene centred around its university, and party animals will be spoiled for choice in the Zona de Las Tascas area of the city. People of all ages gather around the streets near the Campus de la Merced to enjoy a drink and a bite to eat in the many bars and restaurants. Calle Enrique Villar and Calle San Ignacio de Loyola are right in the thick of the action.

10 Old Town (El Barrio), Alicante

MAP U2

Every street and narrow lane in Alicante's atmospheric old quarter is packed solid with bars and clubs, which start late and don't stop until dawn. The birthplace of Alicante's nightlife, the bars here are popular with both university students and older people. There's a good mix of styles and venues, with something to suit most tastes and age groups.

Cafes lining a street in Old Town

TOP 10 TIPS FOR CLUBBERS

Wine and tapas

1 Don't Arrive Too Early
Be prepared for a very late night. Dinner is eaten late, so the clubs in Spain rarely get going before 1am.

2 Dress to Impress
Take some trouble over your appearance; local clubbers make a big effort. Note that many clubs don't allow trainers (sports shoes).

3 El Tramnochador
A special tram service between Alicante and El Campello runs all through the night on Fridays and Saturdays in July and August.

4 Free Drinks
Club admission prices usually include one drink at the bar, so make sure that you keep hold of your ticket.

5 Flyers
You can get flyers on special one-off musical events from local music shops.

6 Terrazas
Many of the clubs on the Costa Blanca have outdoor terraces, which offer welcome respite from the heat and rigours of the dance floor.

7 Discounts
Competition between clubs is fierce, so watch out for flyers offering discounts or free entry.

8 Drugs
Drugs may be offered to you, but they are illegal in Spain, and the penalties for possession are tough.

9 Special Events
You can get information about special clubbing events at www.clubbing spain.com (in Spanish only).

10 Beach Parties
Beach parties are common, free and entirely spontaneous.

Culinary Highlights

1 Embutidos (Charcuterie)
The dry air of the inland regions is used to cure the products from the annual pig slaughter. These include sausages, hams, morcilla (blood sausage) and various types of chorizo (spicy sausage).

2 Fish and Seafood
Excellent fish and seafood is caught fresh and served all along the Costa Blanca and the Costa Cálida. Both Dénia and the Mar Menor are renowned for their prawns. *Dorada a la sal* (sea bream baked in rock salt) is a delicious fish dish found on the menus of more expensive restaurants.

Grilled lamb chops

Whole sea bream

3 Orxata (Horchata)
Orxata is a sweet, creamy drink made from ground *chufas* (tiger-nuts). It's tastier and more refreshing than it might sound. Alicante produces a variation made with almonds. In summer, it's delicious served with crushed ice. Look out for the sign "*artesanal*", meaning homemade. These varieties are much better than the bottled kind.

4 Meat and Game
The mountainous interior behind the coasts produces excellent local meat and game. Many dishes feature *conejo* (rabbit), *liebre* (hare), *perdiz* (partridge) or *codorniz* (quail). One very reliable dish is *chuletas de cordero* (lamb chops), grilled, barbecued or roasted.

5 Fruit and Vegetables
The benign climate of Eastern Spain makes for a long growing season and a plentiful supply of fruit and vegetables. Oranges and lemons are grown in the northern Costa Blanca. The town of Callosa d'en Sarrià specializes in tart *nísperos* (medlars). Olives, almonds and grapes all come in many varieties.

6 Paella and other Rice Dishes
The best paella – *arroz* (rice) with chicken, rabbit, beans and other vegetables – is cooked over a wood fire. There is also a seafood version. Other tasty rice dishes are *arroz negro* (cooked in squid ink) and *arroz a banda* (cooked in fish stock). Rice grown in Calasparra in Murcia has its own *denominación de origen*.

Seafood paella

Costa Blanca's classic nougat, *turrón*

7 Turrón
Anyone with a sweet tooth will be in heaven in the Costa Blanca, which is famous for *turrón*, the delicious local nougat made with honey and nuts. There are two different kinds: a soft version called "Xixona" (Jijona), after the biggest producer of *turrón*, and the crunchier "Alicante".

8 Stews
Even the cheapest menu in the region is likely to include a hearty meat or fish and vegetable stew as a main course for a winter lunchtime. It may be described as *puchero*, *cocido*, *caldero* or *olla* – after a traditional earthenware cook pot – and the exact recipe might change according to market availability.

9 Local Wine
The characteristic wines of Alicante (Monóvar) and Murcia (Jumilla and Yecla) are robust reds best drunk young. Whites are more likely to be sweet dessert wines such as mistela from Teulada. Bullas, however, produces a refreshing rosé for summer drinking.

10 Chocolate
Museo de Chocolate Valor: Pianista Gonzalo Soriano, 13
■ www.valor.es
The seaside town of La Vila Joiosa (Villajoyosa) has been making chocolate for three centuries. A museum *(see p82)* devoted to it is run by Valor, one of the biggest chocolate-makers in Spain.

TOP 10 VEGETARIAN DISHES

1 Tortilla de patata (or española)
The classic Spanish tortilla (omelette) is made with fried potatoes and onions and sliced like a cake.

2 Bocadillo de queso
The ultimate standby: a sandwich made from half a baguette sliced and filled with Manchego cheese.

3 Patatas bravas
Spicy fried chunks of potato are made all the more delicious when dipped in *alioli* (garlic mayonnaise) or spicy tomato sauce.

4 Berenjenas fritas
Aubergines sliced, dipped in egg and flour and fried. Excellent with honey drizzled over the top.

5 Escalivada
Smoky grilled vegetables – most typically aubergine and red pepper – served with olive oil.

6 Pan con tomate
This simple, delicious dish consists of toasted bread spread liberally with crushed tomato and sprinkled with olive oil and salt. A great choice for breakfast or a mid-morning snack.

7 Gazpacho andaluz
A cold vegetable soup – featuring blended tomato, cucumber and garlic – available mainly in summer.

8 Espinacas con garbanzos
A stew made with spinach, chick peas and usually onion and garlic.

9 Ensalada
Spanish salads are generous and pretty varied, and can usually be customized to order.

10 Menestra and Pisto
Hearty mixed vegetable stews – but check that ham hasn't been added before you order.

***Pisto* (mixed vegetable stew)**

🔟 Tapas

Selection of traditional Spanish tapas

1 Nuts and Crisps

With so many almond trees just inland, it's not surprising that the best *almendras* (almonds) turn up shelled, skinned and toasted on bartops as an instant snack. Alternatively, you may be served a portion of *cacahuetes* (peanuts) still in their shells. *Papas* (Spanish crisps), deep fried in olive oil, are also tasty.

2 Albóndigas (Meatballs)

Lean meat (usually beef) is formed into balls with soggy bread, sautéed and then bathed in a rich and often spicy tomato sauce. Along with other tapas, you'll usually find *albóndigas* in a dish in a heated display cabinet on the top of the bar.

Albóndigas in tomato sauce

3 Croquetas (Croquettes)

Finely chopped fish, ham, chicken, mushrooms or spinach is stirred into a béchamel sauce made so thick that it can be formed into oblong shapes, which are then coated with breadcrumbs and deep fried. Croquetas are served hot – just tell the person serving you how many you can eat.

4 Aceitunas or Olivas (Olives)

The fruit of the ubiquitous olive tree is pounded and split, soaked to remove some of the bitterness and marinated in garlic and herbs. Sometimes olives come stuffed with anchovies.

5 Chorizo (Sausage)

Spain's national sausage is fat, orange- or scarlet-coloured, made from chopped pork, and flavoured with a mild, sweet variety of chilli. It is normally eaten cold, sliced but some varieties are fried.

6 Tortilla (Omelette)

An egg-only omelette is known as a *tortilla francesa* but a staple of Spanish cuisine adds vegetables to the eggs to make a thick cake served in slices with bread. *Tortilla murciana* is made with tomatoes and peppers.

7 Queso (Cheese)

The most common cheese in tapas bars is Manchego, made from sheep's milk in La Mancha in central Spain. The tastiest variety is *curado* (mature). You may also be offered soft, fresh cheese with a more subtle taste.

8 Montaditos

A typical tapa of eastern Spain are *montaditos*, the word meaning "one thing on top of another". These are mini baguette rolls sliced open and piled with a variety of fillings from the obvious to the wildly creative. They are usually served warm to be eaten in two or three mouthfuls immediately.

9 Ensaladilla Rusa (Russian Salad)

It has been said that this mixture of diced cooked potatoes, peas, olives, mayonnaise and usually tuna fish should be called "Spanish national salad" but its name has, for some reason, stuck. Eaten cold, a small portion may sometimes be served as a garnish to another tapa.

10 Jamón Serrano (Ham)

Cooked ham is known as *jamón de York* but it bears no comparison with the dry-cured "mountain ham", which is one of the famous delicacies of Spain. The best bars keep a leg of it mounted on a stand and will thinly slice it off the bone to order. The finest varieties almost melt in your mouth.

Jamón serrano hanging in a shop

TOP 10 SEAFOOD TAPAS

Pescaíto frito is a tasty tapas dish

1 Pescaíto frito
Mixed fish – whole or in pieces – that has been dipped in flour and deep fried.

2 Calamares (squid)
Often prepared a *la romana* (in battered rings) but may be *en su tinta* (cooked in its own ink).

3 Sepia (cuttlefish)
Small cuttlefish called *chopitos* or *puntillas* are battered and fried and served with a lemon slice.

4 Mejillones (mussels)
May be served in vinaigrette or *escabeche* (a spicy pickled marinade).

Tapa of *mejillones*

5 Pulpo (octopus)
Chewy morsels of octopus may be served in vinaigrette or *a la plancha* (grilled).

6 Gambas and langostinos (prawns)
Prawns come in a variety of sizes and serving styles, such as popular *gambas al ajillo* – prawns fried with garlic.

7 Boquerones (anchovies)
Tasty small fish most commonly eaten cold, in vinegar, but can also be fried.

8 Sardinas (sardines)
Typically served barbecued until the skin just starts to become crisp.

9 Salpicón de mariscos
An aromatic sauce of seafood, tomatoes, garlic, onions and herbs.

10 Berberechos or almejas (clams)
The best ones are cooked still in their shells in a white wine and herb sauce.

⑩ Restaurants

① La Finca, Elx (Elche)

This beautiful restaurant set in lush gardens offers traditional Mediterranean recipes with an innovative touch; the *menú de degustación* offers the opportunity to taste a range of chef Susi Díaz's most popular creations. There's also a fantastic wine cellar *(see p97)*.

② Restaurante d'Almansa, Cartagena

Thanks to a winning combination of delicious local fare served with a contemporary twist, this elegant restaurant comes highly recommended by locals. The staff are charming and the prices very reasonable. Try the tuna tataki with stir-fried vegetables and coconut ajo blanco, or the lobster and prawn rice *(see p107)*.

③ Casa Pepa, Ondara

Set in a 19th-century building surrounded by attractive vegetable gardens, orange trees and olive groves, Casa Pepa is justifiably proud of its coveted Michelin star. Try one of the tasting menus, paired with excellent wines. Booking ahead is essential *(see p87)*.

④ El Misteri d'Anna, Elx

A stylish but homely restaurant set in a house in a quiet residential area, El Misteri d'Anna serves spectacular fresh Spanish and Mediterranean dishes, which are ornately presented. With three distinct dining rooms and a beautiful garden terrace, this is the perfect choice for a celebratory dinner *(see p97)*.

One of three elegant dining rooms at El Misteri d'Anna, Elx

from the Mar Menor (including cod in *pil-pil* sauce), as well as locally reared meats, which are grilled to perfection. Old-fashioned in the best sense of the word, it offers impeccable service and a splendid, rather formal setting. There's also a tapas bar with an outdoor dining area, and on the lower floor is La Muralla, a café by the city's ancient Arab wall (see p113).

Piripi restaurant interior, Alicante

5 Piripi, Alicante (Alacant)

Smart and stylish, Piripi serves some of the finest traditional rice dishes in the whole city. Try the delectable *arroz con sepionet y alcachofas*, cooked with baby squid and artichokes, but be sure to save room for the pleasant home-made desserts too. Piripi's tapas bar is one of the best in town (see p97).

6 Govana, Alicante

Enjoying a strong local reputation for its combination of tradition and creativity, this family-run restaurant serves superb Mediterranean seafood and rice dishes, using fresh local produce and classic recipes. A great wine list complements the delicious menu (see p97).

7 Rincón de Pepe, Murcia

Set in the Tryp by Windham Rincón de Pepe hotel, this is the plushest restaurant in Murcia City. It serves exquisitely prepared fresh seafood

8 Batiste, Santa Pola

Overlooking the port, this large, airy restaurant is a great place to try some of Costa Blanca's famous rice dishes or *fideuá* (Valencian paella) with black rice. It also serves classic seafood and shell-fish plates with fresh catches from Santa Pola bay (see p97).

9 Quique Dacosta Restaurante, Dénia (Denia)

Dynamic young chef Quique Dacosta gives traditional Spanish rice dishes a creative twist at this restaurant with a breezy terrace. The fabulous dishes on the tasting menus are presented with precision and flair, making them almost too beautiful to eat. With its three Michelin stars, this haut cuisine establishment is the best place in town to try Dénia's famous prawns (see p87).

Paella-style dish, Quique Dacosta, Dénia

10 Casa de los Musso, Lorca

This historic restaurant, located in the centre of Lorca, has several cosy dining areas where you can enjoy creative Spanish cuisine. The appetizing meals are prepared from meticulously sourced regional ingredients by the skilled chef. There is a great selection of wine, and the tasting menu is particularly good value (see p115).

TOP 10 Costa Blanca for Free

The tiled Explanada promenade along the harbour in Alicante

1 On the Streets

In Alicante (Alacant) La Explanada *(see p16)* promenade and the streets and squares of El Barrio, are great places to stroll around and people-watch from a café at almost any time of day or night. Benidorm *(see p48)* and the town of Altea *(see p48)* are also good for street life.

2 Reach for the Sky

www.visitbenidorm.es/ver/1300/benidorms-skyline
Benidorm has a useful guide on its tourist website giving details of all sky-scrapers over 100 m (328 ft) or 25 floors in the city. It's in Spanish but is highly visual. Choose your viewpoint – the *mirador* in the old town; *La Cruz* (the Cross) monument in the hills above Levante beach; or Tossal de la Cala hill by Poniente beach – and see how many skyscrapers you can identify.

3 Back to Nature

Visiting a nature reserve, such as Calblanque *(see pp12–13)*, on the coast of Murcia, or the Sierra Espuña *(see pp26–7)* inland, can easily take up a whole day without costing anything. Dress appropri-ately, and take water and a picnic.

4 Benidorm Arts

Benidorm town council's Department of Culture sponsors a busy season of free arts events all year round. Every two months it publishes a guide to what's coming up; you can collect one at the town hall or a tourist information office *(see p123)*. The lively programme includes a wide range of theatre, exhibitions, concerts and workshops.

5 Visit Guadalest

The castle and museums of Guadalest *(see pp18–19)* charge admission but you can stroll around the rest of this picturesque mountain village for free, enjoying the views and taking pictures. You can also dip into the folk museum, which asks visitors only for a voluntary donation.

6 Mud Bathing in the Mar Menor

The mud in one corner of the Mar Menor (outside San Pedro del Pinatar, on the way to the Punta de Algas) is said to have health-giving properties *(see p101)*. Take a bucket to scoop it up and smear it on you, before washing off in the sea. It's pungent stuff so wear an old swimming costume.

7 Join the Party

There's a fiesta going on somewhere practically all year. If you hear firecrackers, head that way. Most fiestas have a spectacular outdoor public centrepiece, the best being the Holy Week celebrations in Lorca, Alcoi's Moors and Christians processions in April and the Hogueras de San Juan in Alicante in June (see pp74–5).

8 Climb the Penyal d'Ifac

This great limestone rock is yours to enjoy during daylight hours. Get there early to avoid the crowds and spend the morning climbing to the summit some 332 m (1,089 ft) above the resort of Calp. The Penyal (see pp20–21) is rightly the iconic symbol of the Costa Blanca.

9 Among the Palm Groves
www.visitelche.com

The city of Elx (Elche) is one big palm tree grove – El Palmeral. The Horta de Cura garden charges entry but the rest of the trees just merge with the street plan. Ask the tourist office for the guided walk leaflet or download it from the Visit Elche website.

Palm tree groves in Elx

10 Churches and Cathedrals

Churches in the region are free to visit. Start with Murcia's great Baroque Catedral de Santa María (see pp34–5). Bigger churches have opening hours but in small towns and villages the church is normally kept locked and you will have to ask for the key in the local bar or shop.

TOP 10 BUDGET TIPS

Café in Alicante old town

1 Have coffee at the bar inside a café. It may well be cheaper than drinking at an outdoor table.

2 Look out for last-minute bargains for all-inclusive package holidays.

3 *Casas rurales* (self-catering village houses) can be great value if you don't mind being a few kilometres away from the coast.

4 Visit off season to get the very best deals for flights and hotels.

5 Hire a bike and do some cycling. There are hire shops in Alicante, Murcia, Benidorm and elsewhere.

6 On weekday lunchtimes order the *menú del día*: an inexpensive set menu offered by many restaurants.

7 Ask around. The locals will know the best and cheapest restaurants.

8 Some museums offer free admission at certain times, or on a certain day of the week, month or even year.

9 Make use of small local shops. It can be easy to spend more than you intend in a big supermarket.

10 Use public transport. You can get to most of the well-known sights by bus, tram or train from Alicante.

Tram in Alicante

Festivals and Events

1 Carnavales (Carnival)
Feb

Carnival is a chance to let off steam before Lent, and there are wild parties across the region. Pego village in the north puts on a good show, but the best of all is in Águilas (see p103).

Holy Week procession in Lorca

2 Semana Santa (Holy Week)
Mar/Apr

Every town has parades in Holy Week, but the Murcia region is famous for its dazzling celebrations. Processions in Murcia City, Cartagena, Mula, Lorca and Moratalla are all famous, but those in Alicante (Alacant) and Orihuela are also well worth seeing.

3 Moros y Cristianos (Moors and Christians)
Usually end Apr

Mock battles between Moors and Christians have been held for centuries. The most famous one takes place in Alcoi (Alcoy) around the end of April, but most villages have their own version.

4 Fiesta de los Caballos del Vino (Festival of the Knights of Wine)
2 May

According to a medieval legend, the Knights Templar broke out of the besieged castle in Caravaca de la Cruz (see p109) on a desperate search for water, but all they could find was wine. The story is recalled on 2 May each year, when richly dressed horses and horsemen form a procession from the castle, and local wine is blessed.

5 Las Hogueras de San Juan (Bonfires of Saint John)
20–24 Jun

The Feast of St John is celebrated in June with bonfires, fireworks and parades across the region. Alicante's festival is the biggest (see p17).

6 La Mar de Músicas
Jul ■ www.lamardemusicas.com

Held every July in Cartagena, this world music festival has become one of the best of its kind in Europe. Concerts take place in the town hall square, the ancient cathedral, and several other beautiful settings around the old quarter.

Mock battle re-enactment in Alcoi

(7) Certamen de las Habaneres (Festival of Habaneras)

Late Jul ■ www.habaneras.org

Habaneras are plaintive sea shanties, which get their name from the Cuban city where many Spaniards went to seek their fortunes – Havana. Torrevieja hosts a prestigious competition annually in late July.

(8) Bous a la Mar (Bulls in the Sea)

First fortnight of Aug

The climax of Dénia's summer festival is the Bous a la Mar, when bulls are sent down the streets, with brave locals in pursuit; it's the locals, rather than the bulls, who end up in the sea!

Medieval mystery play in Elx

(9) Misteri d'Elx (Elche) (Mystery of Elx)

Mid-Aug

The origins of this medieval mystery play – the only one to survive a 17th-century ban by the Council of Trent – date back to the 13th century. It is performed each year in the Basílica de Santa María, Elx *(see p91)*.

(10) Fira de Tots Sants (All Saints Fair)

1 Nov

Cocentaina has celebrated All Saints every year since 1346. Originally an agricultural and grain market, it is now a hugely popular medieval-style fair selling all kinds of local produce.

TOP 10 TIPS FOR VISITING FIESTAS

People gathering for a fiesta

1 Get there early
Events generally start at the time advertised, and you'll get a better view the earlier you arrive.

2 Plan your route
Some streets are likely to be closed during a fiesta and others may be blocked by crowds, so ask for details in advance and plan ahead.

3 Take a portable chair
There can be a lot of standing and waiting around, and a portable chair can be a life-saver.

4 Pace yourself
It's always wise to chill out and have an afternoon siesta if you are going to be staying up late.

5 Be flexible
Arrangements sometimes change; be ready to go with the flow.

6 Don't take risks
The locals know what they are doing, but you may not, especially when it comes to chasing bulls through narrow town streets, for example.

7 Be respectful
It may seem as though anything goes at a fiesta but a certain standard of behaviour is expected.

8 Take photographs tactfully
Don't interrupt a parade, or the work of the police who are managing an event, just to take a photograph.

9 Be wary of pickpockets
There's not usually much crime during a fiesta but don't let your guard down and take care of your valuables.

10 Don't expect to do anything else
During fiesta, the town shuts down. You'll find that museums, sights and offices are generally closed.

Costa Blanca
Area by Area

**Mountain backdrop to the town of
Altea in Northern Costa Blanca**

TOP10 Northern Costa Blanca

The windswept capes and enticing coves of northern Costa Blanca have attracted settlers for thousands of years, but the trickle became a deluge during the 1960s with the development of modern package holiday resorts. It's not difficult to see the allure of the magnificent coastline, with its jagged cliffs, pale sandy beaches and secret coves of turquoise water, but the coastal strip, nightclubs and holiday resorts are only half the story. Just a few miles inland, remote sierras and lush valleys survive untouched, with traditional whitewashed villages on hilltops, dramatic waterfalls plunging into natural pools and ruined castles and ancient towns recalling an illustrious past.

Cesare Borgia memorial statue, Gandia

1 Alcoi (Alcoy)
MAP E3

The inland industrial town of Alcoi sits beneath the Sierra de Mariola mountain range. Best known for its noisy and spectacular Moros y Cristianos festival held towards the end of April (see p74), it also has a wealth of Modernista houses, especially on two streets, Carrer Sant Nicolau (see p47) and Carrer Sant Llorenç. The municipal archaeological museum has some interesting Iberian finds.

Moros y Cristianos festival, Alcoi

2 Gandia (Gandía)
MAP F2

Gandia's history is inextricably tied up with the Borjas; their opulent Gothic palace home has been impeccably

NORTHERN COSTA BLANCA

- **1** **Top10 Sights**
  see pp79–81
- **1** **Places to Eat**
  see p87
- **1** **Nightlife and Entertainment**
  see p86
- **1** **Views and Picnic Spots**
  see p83
- **1** **Shopping Towns**
  see p82
- **1** **Benidorm Cafés and Restaurants**
  see p85
- **1** **Benidorm Nightlife**
  see p84

restored *(see pp32–3)*. The only other reminder of the town's historic importance is the Gothic church of Santa María. A resort town, Gandía-Playa, has grown up around the port, and has well-manicured beaches *(see p50)*.

③ Xàbia (Jávea)
MAP H3
The bay at Xàbia is perfectly caught between two dramatic capes: the Cap de Sant Antoni and the Cap de la Nau *(see p55)*. The old village of Xàbia, with its narrow streets and fortified medieval church *(see p42)*, is set back from the lively modern resort around the bay.

④ Penyal d'Ifac (Peñón de Ifach)
This huge, jagged rock emerges dramatically from the sea and dominates the entire bay at Calp.

It is connected to the mainland by an isthmus and, although it looks impossibly sheer, there is a fantastic hiking route to the top, which includes a tunnel hewn through part of the rock. The route starts from the visitor's centre at its base *(see pp20–21)*.

The dramatic Penyal d'Ifac

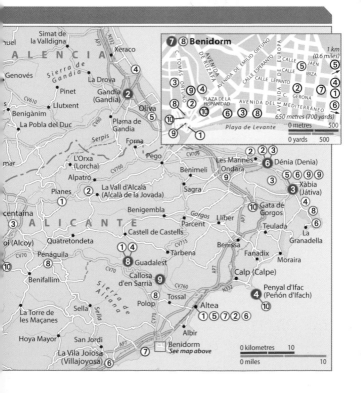

5 Villena
MAP C4

The large, prosperous town of Villena is crowned by a storybook castle, with a medieval village of tile-roofed houses at its feet. The central square is surrounded by 16th-century palaces and the graceful Renaissance church of Santa María, with its flamboyant Baroque façade. The finest palace is now the town hall and a museum containing the Tesoro de Villena, a hoard of Bronze Age gold discovered by chance in the 1960s (see p40).

The Bronze-Age Tesoro de Villena

6 Dénia (Denia)
MAP H2

Now a popular family resort, Dénia was once a sizeable Roman settle-ment. There's a lofty castle, a pretty old quarter huddled around the port, and some great beaches: the family-friendly sands to the north, and a lovely, cove-pocked stretch called Les Rotes to the south (see p50). The strange, bald peak of Montgó looms above the town, perfect for hiking (see p61) and picnicking (see p54).

THE LOVELORN GIANT

There's a curious notch "missing" from the spiky mountains behind Benidorm. According to legend, it was torn out and tossed into the bay by a despairing giant who had been told that his beloved would die by the time the sun set. In so doing he gave her a few moments more of life; the rock became the Isla de Benidorm (see p54).

7 Benidorm
MAP G4

Until the mid-1950s Benidorm was a small sardine fishing village with only a few Spanish tourists. Then, an ambitious plan to maximize the available space within reach of the shoreline was passed. The result is the huge number of high-rises creating the resort's skyline today. Benidorm's success is based not only on two long sandy beaches on either side of the old town – Levante and Poniente (see p50) – but on a policy of catering for tourists of all ages year-round. From tea dances in cafés to techno in nightclubs: Benidorm has something for everyone.

During the day, away from the beach, there isn't much to see, but a walk out to the Balcony of the Mediterranean viewpoint is a must and the Neo-classical Parc de l'Aigüera, with its amphitheatre, is a quiet green place to stroll around. Best for escaping the crowds is a walk up the head-land of the Sierra Helada. Offshore is a small island shaped like a slice of cake dipping into the sea; it can be visited on a boat trip from the harbour.

Dénia's pretty harbourside

8 Guadalest

Perched high on a crag among inland mountain peaks, the white-washed village of Guadalest is the most picturesque spot on the Costa Blanca. Popular sights include the castle, the church belfry and some quirky museums *(see pp18–19)*.

9 Callosa d'en Sarrià and Fonts d'Algar

MAP G3

Just outside of the modest village of Callosa d'en Sarrià are the lovely waterfalls and natural swimming pools of the Fonts d'Algar *(see p54)*. Excellent walking trails lead from here to the Sierra de Bernia.

The hilltop castle at Xàtiva

10 Xàtiva (Játiva)

MAP E1

This ancient mountain town is known as the "City of Two Popes" – Alexander VI and Calixto III (both members of the Borja family) were born here. Piled steeply on a hillside, the narrow streets and arcaded squares are still scattered with handsome churches and escutcheoned mansions, which attest to its medieval importance. It's topped with a fine castle offering incredible views *(see also p45)*.

A MORNING IN XÀTIVA

This walk is best done on a Tuesday or Friday, when the market is held. A castle has sat on the lofty promontory above the town of Xàtiva since Iberian times. Start your morning – before the sun gets too hot – with the stiff climb up to the castle (signposted "castell"), or take the easy option of the little tourist train, which runs from outside the tourist office. From the castle ramparts, the lovely Old City unfolds at your feet, surrounded by endless sierras. One of the finest castles in the region, this is a sublime setting for an annual summer music festival.

On the way down, you can stop for refreshment in the gardens of the charming **Hostería de Mont Sant** *(see p87)*. When you reach the main town, continue down Calle las Santas and turn right onto Calle Roca for the **Museo de l'Almudí** *(see p41)*. It has an excellent collection of archaeological finds and paintings (including some by Xàtiva-born artist José de Ribera). If you are in Xàtiva on a Tuesday or Friday, head down to the nearby Plaza del Mercado, where stalls selling everything from clothes to pots and pans are set out under ancient arcades. Walk up to the Calle Corretgeria and visit the huge **Colegiata Basílica de Santa María** *(see p42)*, still unfinished after more than 400 years. Opposite the basilica is the beautiful Hospital Real (now local administration offices), with a dazzling, exquisitely sculpted Gothic façade. For lunch, try the traditional **La Borda de Lola** *(C/La Reina 13; 657 80 53 75)*.

See map on pp78–9

Shopping Towns

Quirky gift shop in Guadalest

1 Guadalest

Set on a clifftop, Guadalest (see pp18–19) is packed with souvenir shops, offering delicate, handmade lace tablecloths, woollen blankets, slippers and traditional capes. You'll also find a good range of local produce, from liqueurs to honey.

2 Altea
MAP G4

The pretty village of Altea (see p48) was "discovered" by artists during the 1960s and 1970s, and is now filled with galleries and craft shops selling everything from watercolours to pottery and handmade jewellery.

3 Xixona (Jijona)
MAP E4

Xixona (see p46) is the biggest producer of the delicious Spanish turrón (nougat), which is traditionally eaten by locals at Christmas, but is available all year round at countless shops throughout the town.

Turrón (Spanish nougat)

4 Ibi
MAP E4

Ibi's long tradition of making tin toys is sadly now being supplanted by cheap plastics, but there are still some pretty replicas of old-fashioned toys to be found, as well as a selection of more modern electronic and educational toys.

5 Ontinyent
MAP E2

The delightful mountain town of Ontinyent has been producing textiles since Arabic times, and its high-quality wool blankets are exported around the world. There are numerous factory outlets here offering excellent bargains.

6 La Vila Joiosa (Villajoyosa)
MAP F4

La Vila Joiosa (see p49) has been making chocolate since the 17th century. You can buy the perfect souvenir at the famous Valor chocolate factory on the outskirts of town.

7 Alcoi (Alcoy)

This town (see p78) is famous for traditional sweets first introduced by the Arabs. Most cake shops sell sugared almonds and the tasty sugar-coated pine nuts called peladillas.

8 Benidorm

Brash, brazen Benidorm (see p48) is the place to go if you're looking for kitsch souvenirs. It's also a great place to find cheap T-shirts and an enormous variety of beachwear to suit all tastes and budgets.

9 Xàbia (Jávea)

There are two distinct shopping areas here: the old town is a sedate cluster of streets with several unusual shops. In the modern resort set around the waterfront, the shops are much more functional (see p79).

10 Gata de Gorgos
MAP G3

The little inland village of Gata de Gorgos is crammed with shops selling traditional wicker and straw crafts, from garden furniture to baskets and wonderful floppy hats.

See map on pp78–9

Views and Picnic Spots

 Barranc de l'Encantà
MAP F3

The track for the Barranc de l'Encantà is signposted just before Planes. It twists down to the "Ravine of the Enchanted One", a perfect picnic spot, where a waterfall tumbles into a natural swimming pool.

 Adzubieta
MAP F3

The romantic dry-stone ruins of this ancient Arabic village close to La Vall d'Alcalà (Alcalà de la Jovada) in the Vall de Gallinera are great for picnics. A stiff path leads to the rocky peak of La Foradada for amazing views.

 Peak of Montgó
MAP H2

Take the long but not too arduous trail through Montgó Natural Park (see p60) to the top of the mountain for spectacular views over the scrubland and rugged cliff.

 Embalse de Guadalest
MAP F3

This huge, deep blue reservoir at the foot of the valley overlooked by the picturesque village of Guadalest is a wonderful place to stop for a picnic after a hard morning's sightseeing.

 Cap de Sant Antoni
MAP H2

The lighthouse at the tip of the windy Cape of Sant Antoni affords gorgeous views over wave-battered cliffs and the pretty resort of Xàbia (Jávea) curled around the bay.

6 Cap de la Nau (Cabo de la Nao)
MAP H3

Rounding off the southern end of the bay at Xàbia, the Cap de la Nau (see p55) is dotted with well-marked miradors (viewing points).

7 Banyeres de Mariola

There is a lovely picnic and camping area on the outskirts of Banyeres, on the road to Biar. From there you can enjoy great views over the village and its Arab castle (see p45), or take a stroll along the river.

8 Jardín de Santos, Penàguila
MAP F3

These immaculate 19th-century gardens on the edge of the dreamy mountain village of Penàguila are the idyllic setting for a popular barbecue area with picnic tables.

9 Xàtiva (Játiva) Castle
MAP E1

Xàtiva's lofty castle offers beautiful views over the quiet mountain town, with its tiled rooftops and slender spires, and out across endless mountains fading into the distance.

10 Penyal d'Ifac (Peñón de Ifach) Summit Mirador

The mirador at the summit of the Penyal d'Ifac (see pp20–21) is the ultimate viewing point – but you'll have to work to get there, as it's a stiff and slippery 45-minute climb from the base.

View from Cap de Sant Antoni

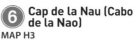

Benidorm Nightlife

1 Rockerfellas
MAP G4 ■ C/Gerona 36

One of Benidorm's original cabaret bars, Rockerfellas is also known for hosting excellent tribute acts and quality comedians.

2 Churchill's
MAP G4 ■ C/Lepanto 14

A firm favourite with the Brits, this raucous pub hosts legendary karaoke nights, which pack in the punters, plus theme nights and lots of competitions. Tacky but fun, in true Benidorm style.

3 Penélope Beach Club
MAP G4 ■ Avda de Alcoi 10 ■ 965 86 33 60 ■ www.penelope benidorm.com

This beachfront outpost of the mega-club Penélope is an elegant bar-cum-club serving classic cocktails.

4 Jokers
MAP G4 ■ Avda Fillipinas (corner of Leptano) ■ 606 88 04 51

This fun and friendly club offers a little bit of everything to please everyone. The club is popular for its live tribute acts dedicated to icons such as Lady Gaga and Bob Marley. The Meatloaf tribute act performs every night *(see p64)*.

5 Benidorm Palace
MAP G4 ■ Avda Severo Ochoa 13 ■ 965 85 16 60 ■ www.benidormpalace.com

Come here for the biggest, flashiest and most extravagant shows in town, featuring acrobats, cabaret singers and show girls.

6 KU Lounge café
MAP G4 ■ Ctra Alicante-Valencia, Km 121 ■ 629 94 17 99 ■ www.kubenidorm.es

A classic nightspot in Benidorm, KU Lounge café is definitely one of the places to see and to be seen.

7 Sinatra's
MAP G4 ■ C/Lepanto 22 ■ 965 86 28 49

This celebrated cocktail bar features regular cabaret and other live acts, and attracts a more mature clientele.

8 Daytona
MAP G4 ■ Avda Alcoi s/n

This motorcycle bar is on Levante beach and serves up American food as well as live rock music until late.

9 La Oveja Negra
MAP G4 ■ C/Los Naranjos 4 ■ 966 29 17 66

Popular with the locals, this tapas bar, which plays a variety of rock music, is a good place to grab a bite and start your night out.

10 Klee Kafee Showbar
MAP G4 ■ C/del Pal 9 ■ 619 93 47 88 ■ Closed Mon & Tue, Aug

This is Benidorm's longest running drag cabaret bar. From 10pm onwards, Miss Tina Gloss hosts an evening of comedy and sing along.

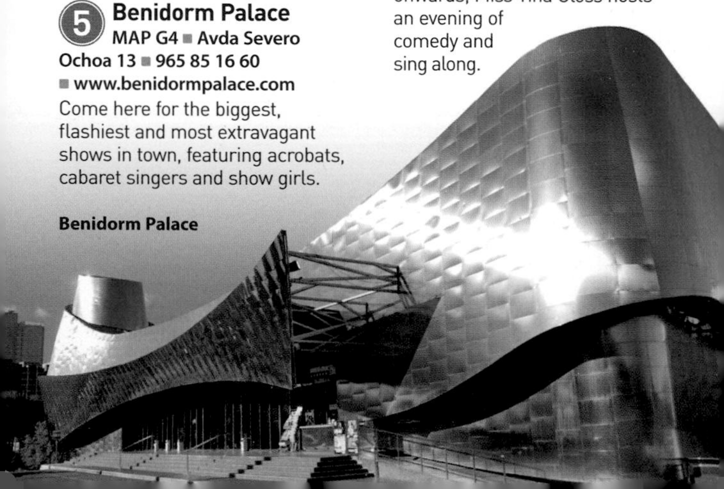

Benidorm Palace

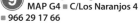

Benidorm Cafés and Restaurants

PRICE CATEGORIES

For a three-course meal for one with half a bottle of wine (or equivalent meal), taxes and extra charges.

€ under €30 €€ €30–50 €€€ over €50

Uptown
MAP G6 ■ C/Mayor 18
■ 966 83 08 51 ■ €

This pretty little restaurant in the old town with a charming terrace specializes in gourmet burgers, presented between slabs of focaccia bread.

2 La Mejillonera
MAP G6 ■ Paseo de la Carretera 16 ■ 628 24 21 99 ■ €

Friendly and rustically decorated, La Mejillonera specializes in its namesake mussels cooked in a variety of ways. It serves other seafood too, including grilled sardines, and a choice of rice dishes such as paella.

3 El Pulpo Pirata
MAP G6 ■ C/Tomás Ortuño 59
■ 966 80 32 19 ■ €

Serving decent Spanish fare, including a superb selection of tapas, cold cuts and cheese. They also serve a great value *menú del día* (set lunch).

4 Aitona
MAP G4 ■ C/Ruzafa 2
■ 965 85 30 10 ■ €€

One of the best places in town to try a traditional paella, this brightly lit restaurant is a favourite with locals and tourists alike. It also serves tasty, simply grilled local meat.

5 Casa Toni
MAP G4 ■ Avda Cuenca, Edificio Gemelo 4 ■ 966 80 12 32
■ Closed Sun D, Mon (except in Jul & Aug) ■ €€

This smart restaurant serves impeccable local rice and seafood dishes, but it's the tapas bar that really pulls in the crowds.

6 Curry Leaf
MAP G4 ■ C/Berlin 1
■ 602 82 89 44 ■ Closed L ■ €

Located near Levante beach, this restaurant serves spicy curries and Tandoori meals in an elegant setting.

7 Ulia
MAP G4 ■ Avda Vicente Llorca Alos 15 ■ 965 85 68 28
■ Closed Sun & Mon D ■ €€

Always busy, Ulia serves up simply prepared fresh fish and local rice dishes on its seafront terrace.

Freshly grilled sardines and salad

8 La Sidrería Aurrera
MAP G4 ■ C/Santo Domingo s/n
■ 618 13 18 73 ■ €

A superb selection of meat and fish is served at this traditional rustic restaurant. Choose from the menu of the day for a superb-value meal.

9 La Rana
MAP G4 ■ Costera del Barco 6
■ 965 86 81 20 ■ €

Enjoy delicious tapas at the bar, or tasty seafood, grilled meats and other creative dishes in the dining room.

La Cava Aragonesa
MAP G4 ■ Plaza de la Constitución 2 ■ 966 80 12 06 ■ €

There are dozens of tapas bars along this street. This one serves a huge range and is incredibly popular, so expect to find standing room only.

See map on pp78–9

Nightlife and Entertainment

1 La Mascarada, Altea

MAP G4 ▪ Plaza Iglesia 8
▪ 692 15 62 77

This bar is worth a visit, if only for the eclectic decor. A vast array of masks and other unique adornments set the atmosphere for the delicious cocktails.

2 Paddy O'Connell, Dénia (Denia)
MAP H2 ▪ C/La Mar 20 ▪ 965 78 48 70

Irish pub with four seating areas, including an outdoor terrace. There is live music from Thursday to Saturday.

3 Jamaica Inn, Dénia
MAP H2 ▪ Carrer Bellavista 9
▪ 966 42 45 93

A good place to watch yachts pulling into their dock. This bar is perfect for enjoying a drink by the ocean.

4 Bacarrá, Gandia (Gandía)
MAP F2 ▪ Carrer de Legazpí 7
▪ 676 17 92 90 ▪ www.bacarra
gandia.com

Bacarrá's "disco-garden" is the place to be during the hot summer months. Events range from DJs to live gigs, go-go dancers and one-off theme parties.

Altea's Palau Altea cultural centre

5 Palau Altea, Altea

MAP G4 ▪ C/Alcoi 18 ▪ 965 84 33 59 ▪ www.palaualtea.com

Altea's main cultural centre features a variety of regular performances of opera, *zarzuela* (typical Spanish operetta), theatre, dance and classical music, as well as jazz, flamenco and pop concerts.

Popular La Esquina, Xàbia

6 La Esquina, Xàbia (Jávea)
MAP H3 ▪ Avda Marina Española 25
▪ 965 79 23 06

Café by day and cocktail bar by night, La Esquina has a beachfront terrace with huge parasols, funky white arm-chairs and sofas. It offers romantic sea views by candlelight at dusk.

7 La Plaza, Altea
MAP G4 ▪ Plaza de la Iglesia 12
▪ 965 84 26 30

This mellow cocktail bar on the village's prettiest square sometimes has live jazz, blues and soul events.

8 Achill, Xàbia
MAP H3 ▪ Paseo Amanecer s/n
▪ 965 77 18 18 ▪ www.achilljavea.com

This stylish bar and club with a seafront terrace is good for a quiet cocktail early on, but heats up later.

9 La Llum, Xàbia
MAP H3 ▪ Carrer de Gual 1

Hidden in an old town house, techno and house keep the party going until dawn at popular La Llum.

10 Black Jack Pub, Alcoi (Alcoy)
MAP E3 ▪ Plaza Gonzalo Cantó s/n
▪ 675 52 27 10

Spanish pop and electronic dance music is played at this disco pub kitted out like Vegas in the 1960s.

Places to Eat

1 Mesón El Viscayo, Castalla

MAP D4 ▪ Camino de la Bola s/n ▪ 965 56 01 96 ▪ Closed D ▪ €

This country restaurant with a charming atmosphere makes its own *embutidos* (sausages). It is famous for its delectable gazpachos, and a shepherd's dish made with meat and game.

2 Quique Dacosta, Dénia (Denia)

MAP H2 ▪ C/Rascassa 1 ▪ 965 78 41 79 ▪ Open Mar–Jun & mid-Sep–Feb: Wed–Sun; Jul–mid-Sep: daily ▪ €€€

Try excellent fresh seafood (including Dénia's famous prawns) and local rice dishes, imaginatively prepared at this restaurant with three Michelin stars.

3 L'Escaleta, Cocentaina

MAP E3 ▪ Subida Estación Norte 205 ▪ 965 59 21 00 ▪ Closed Mon, Tue, Sun; Wed & Thu D; third and fourth weeks Jan ▪ €€€

This elegant chalet at the foot of the mountains serves elaborate regional cuisine, including succulent lamb, fresh fish and heavenly desserts.

4 La Bohême, Xàbia (Jávea)

MAP H3 ▪ Paseo David Ferrer, Bloque 1, Local 2 ▪ 965 79 16 00 ▪ €

The selection of fresh tapas is the speciality at this popular seaside spot. Try the fresh seafood and meat dishes.

5 El lloc Restaurante-Pizzeria, Oliva

MAP G2 ▪ C/del Alcalde Juan Sancho 3 ▪ 962 85 08 32 ▪ Closed Tue ▪ €

There is a wide variety of choices here, with excellent pizza, pasta, rice and meat dishes. The menu of the day is usually good value.

6 Sirtaki, Altea

MAP G4 ▪ C/San Pedro 40 ▪ 642 11 15 23 ▪ Closed Wed ▪ €

Enjoy traditional Greek cuisine at this pleasant restaurant with a terrace overlooking the sea.

7 Warynessy, Villena

MAP C4 ▪ C/Isabel la Católica 13 ▪ 965 80 10 47 ▪ Closed Mon ▪ €€

This sleek restaurant and tapas bar in sleepy Villena serves modern twists on traditional Alicantino recipes.

8 Ca l'Angels, Polop

MAP G4 ▪ C/Gabriel Miró 12 ▪ 965 87 02 26 ▪ Closed Tue; mid-Jun–mid-Jul; Sep–mid-Jun: D except Fri, Sat; mid-Jul–Aug: Tue ▪ €€

This welcoming restaurant serves fresh fish and local dishes such as kid with roast garlic.

9 Casa Pepa, Ondara

MAP G2 ▪ Partida Pamís 7–30 ▪ 965 76 66 06 ▪ Closed Mon & Tue, Wed–Sun D ▪ www.capepa.es ▪ €€€

A Michelin-starred restaurant, Casa Pepa has stylishly decorated dining rooms and beautiful gardens.

10 Hostería de Mont Sant, Xàtiva (Játiva)

MAP E1 ▪ Subida al Castillo s/n ▪ 962 27 50 81 ▪ www.mont-sant.com ▪ €€€

Enjoy regional cuisine with a selection of vegetarian dishes in the gardens of this hotel above Xàtiva *(see p126)*.

Hostería de Mont Sant, Xàtiva

See map on pp78–9 ←

TOP10 Southern Costa Blanca

Alicante (Alacant), capital of the Costa Blanca, has an enticing old quarter tumbling down the lower slopes of a vast cliff where a majestic fortress has stood guard for 1,000 years. Modern avenues have great shops and tapas bars. Inland, dry plains give way to mountains riddled with caves and scattered with medieval villages and castles – the region was on the front line between the Arabic and Christian worlds during the Middle Ages. The town of Novelda houses an architectural gem from the more recent past. Along the coastline, long, sandy beaches prevail, and you can escape the crowds on the lovely Isla Tabarca. Heading south, the elegant town of Elx (Elche) is surrounded by ancient palm groves, and Orihuela's affluent history is recalled by a mix of Gothic churches and Renaissance palaces.

Baroque altarpiece, Iglesia de Santas Justa y Rufina

SOUTHERN COSTA BLANCA

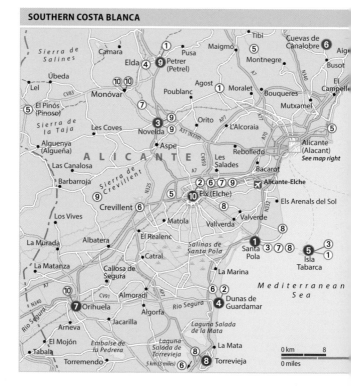

① Santa Pola
MAP E6, Q1

Santa Pola is a cheerful family resort set around a pretty port. At the heart of the village is a sturdy castle built in the 16th century as a defence against pirates. The lighthouse at the tip of the Cape of Santa Pola offers fine views of the coastline and the small island of Tabarca, a short ferry-ride away. The salt lakes on the fringes of the village are now a Natural Park attracting flamingos and other aquatic birds.

② Alicante (Alacant)
The main gateway to the Costa Blanca, this bustling city is often overlooked in the charge to the beaches and resorts, yet this is one of Spain's most engaging cities, with a picturesque old quarter, beautiful churches and fascinating museums, and a lively port with lots of bars and

Colourful tiled house, Alicante

restaurants. The city is dominated by the splendid Castillo de Santa Bárbara (see pp14–17), perched high on a cliff above the sea.

① **Top 10 Sights**
see pp89–91

① **Places to Eat**
see p97

① **Nightlife**
see p96

① **Views and Picnic Spots**
see p93

① **Shopping Towns**
see p92

① **Alicante Tapas Bars**
see p95

① **Alicante Shops**
see p94

3 Novelda
MAP D5

Sleepy Novelda rarely makes it onto tourist itineraries, but it should. This little country town offers some fine Modernista mansions, of which the most impressive is the Casa-Museo Modernista *(see pp22–3)*. On the edge of town, the castle of La Mola squats next to the Gaudí-inspired sanctuary of Saint Mary Magdalene.

4 Dunas de Guardamar
MAP Q2

This wild and lovely stretch of dunes on the outskirts of the low-key tourist enclave of Guardamar is a protected area, which has blocked the intrusion of high-rise developments. The windswept dunes undulate along pale sandy beaches, backed by shady pine glades with walking paths, cycling routes, archaeological remains and picnic areas. Although the beaches are popular in summer, they remain relatively uncrowded *(see p93)*.

The Dunas de Guardamar

5 Isla Tabarca
The island of Tabarca *(see pp30–31)* is just 2 km (1 mile) long and 450 m (492 yards) wide and sits off the coast of Santa Pola. Wild, pebbly coves and bays pucker its shoreline, and its clear waters are now a marine reserve. Regular ferries make the short journey from Santa Pola year-round. They also run from Alicante (Alacant), Benidorm and Guardamar. Many tourists simply make for the seafood restaurants around the port, leaving the little town to more intrepid explorers.

Inside the Cuevas de Canelobre

6 Cuevas de Canelobre
MAP E4 ▪ Busot ▪ 965 69 92 50 ▪ Open Easter week: 10:30am–6:30pm Mon–Fri, 10:30am–3pm Sat & Sun; Jul & Aug: 10:30am–7:30pm daily; Sep–Jun: 10:30am–4:50pm Tue–Fri, 10:30am–5:50pm Sat & Sun ▪ Adm ▪ turismobusot.com

This vast, lofty cavern is the largest and most impressive of a network of caves within the Cabecó d'Or mountain near Busot *(see p62)*.

7 Orihuela
MAP P2

Churches, monasteries and palaces attest to Orihuela's distinguished history. Set back from the coast in a fertile valley, this ancient capital of an Arabic *taifa* became a centre of learning after the Reconquest *(see p38)*, and the Catholic monarchs once held court here. Fine churches to visit include the cathedral, the Colegio de Santo Domingo *(see p43)* and the charming Iglesia de Santas Justa y Rufina.

EMPRESS SISI

The Imperial Palm in the Hort del Cura in Elx (Elche) is named in honour of the Empress Sisi of Austria (1837–98). She was a beautiful and tortured figure who escaped the stifling responsibilities of court life by sailing around the Mediterranean and indulging in unusual beauty treatments, which included bathing in cow's milk.

8 Torrevieja
MAP Q3

This resort town has a lively seafront and unusual rock pools in place of a beach. There's also a huge modern marina offering watersports. On the fringes of the town sit two vast salt lakes – they form a designated nature reserve that attracts several species of birds, both migratory and resident.

9 Petrer (Petrel)
MAP D4

Medieval Petrer is dominated by its impressive castle (see p45). The old town has almost been swallowed by the adjacent (and unlovely) industrial city of Elda. Both share a long shoe-making tradition, and Petrer's streets are still home to traditional cobblers. There's a pretty Neo-Classical church and a pair of charming hermitages.

10 Elx (Elche)
MAP D6, Q1

Alicante province's second city, Elx is dominated by its immense date palm grove, a UNESCO World Heritage Site, part of which is closed off as the Hort del Cura (see pp28–9). Elx was originally sited nearby at La Alcudia. It is here that the famous Dama de Elx was found – the original is now in Madrid. Modern Elx revolves around the Basílica de Santa María, the setting for the Misteri d'Elx (see p75).

Dama de Elx replica, Hort del Cura

A DAY IN TWO CITIES

▶ MORNING

Allow a full day (but avoid Sunday and Monday) for this tour of two elegant but very different cities. Begin in **Orihuela** at the vast **Colegio de Santo Domingo** (see p43), topped with a pastel tower. Stroll to the city centre and peek into the graceful Cathedral de San Salvador, which overlooks a pretty square. Next, walk down Calle Ramón y Cajal lined with terrace cafés and shops, before continuing to the delightful Iglesia de Santas Justa y Rufina, with its unmistakable bell tower. Head back to Plaza del Salvador for lunch at **Bizarre Gastrobar** (865 75 15 12), which serves delicious, hearty traditional dishes.

AFTERNOON

Take the short drive along the A7 motorway to **Elx**, set in famous palm groves. Explore the **Hort del Cura** (see pp28–9), then stroll back to the historic heart of the town and the vast blue-domed **Basílica de Santa María** (see p43). Next to the basilica is a 13th-century watchtower, the Torre de la Calaforra. You can learn more about the famous Misteri d'Elx, one of the last surviving medieval mystery plays regularly performed in Europe, at the nearby Museo de la Festa on Carrer Major de la Vila. Finish with a well-earned drink on the terrace of the **Café África** (Plaza del Congreso Eucarístico) over-looking the basílica.

See maps on pp88–9

Shopping Towns

 Agost
MAP D5

With a long ceramic-making tradition dating back for centuries, Agost has dozens of shops that sell the earthenware water jars (botijos) typical of the region, along with a range of ceramic items from pots to platters.

Local produce on sale in Elx

② Elx (Elche)
Come around Easter to see Elx's famous and elaborate palm crosses being made for the Palm Sunday parades (see p29). At any time of year, dozens of shops sell fresh dates and delicious date sweets and cakes (see p91).

③ Alicante (Alacant)
The ultimate shopping destination, Alicante has the biggest department stores, plus plenty of large high-street chains, all along the Avenida Maisonnave (see pp14–17).

④ Elda
MAP D4

A big, industrial city, Elda is one of the largest shoe-making centres in Spain. Numerous factory outlets on the outskirts of the town offer excellent shoe bargains.

 El Pinós (Pinoso)
MAP C5

This is one of the best-known wine towns in the Alicante region (see p52), but it's also justly famous for its embutidos – delicious cured hams and sausages made with meat from locally reared livestock and prepared to traditional recipes.

⑥ Crevillent
MAP D6

Renowned throughout Spain for its colourful rugs and carpets, Crevillent has dozens of workshops and factories offering top-quality woven products. Other local crafts include glassware and wickerwork.

⑦ Santa Pola
This town's traditional souvenirs are objects made from seashells – a fashion that you may have thought died out in the 1970s. These run the gamut from the downright kitsch to the surprisingly pretty (see p89).

⑧ Torrevieja
Edged with two enormous salt lakes (a designated Natural Park) and pale pyramids of gleaming salt, the town of Torrevieja is a curious sight. Its shops sell unusual carved boats made entirely from salt as well as other salt products (see p91).

⑨ Novelda
This place (see pp22–3) is most famous for its marble, but if that proves difficult to pack in your suitcase, you could always pick up some locally grown golden saffron to flavour your own paellas (see p66) back home instead.

 Monóvar
MAP D5

The jolly wine town of Monóvar (see p52) produces an excellent, robust red wine, as well as refreshing rosés, but it is best known for the wonderful dessert wine El Fondillón.

← See maps on pp88–9

Views and Picnic Spots

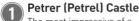 **Petrer (Petrel) Castle**
The most impressive of a line of castles that cuts through the middle of the Alicante region, the sturdy fortifications of Petrer Castle make for a perfect picnic – and, indeed, picture – spot with endless views *(see p91)*.

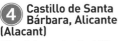 **Dunas de Guardamar**
The protected expanse of undulating dunes *(see p51)* backed by a gnarled pine forest on the edge of Guardamar del Segura makes a delightful place for a picnic.

3 Isla Tabarca
The secluded coves at the western end of this pretty island *(see pp30–31)* are perfect for picnics. If you need to work up an appetite for lunch, you can always go for a swim or a snorkel first.

4 Castillo de Santa Bárbara, Alicante (Alacant)
Alicante's spectacular hilltop castle *(see pp14–15)* dominates the whole city, and its ramparts and terraces offer endless views over the deep blue Mediterranean.

 Tibi Reservoir
MAP E4
Built at the end of the 16th century, and perfectly slotted into a narrow gorge, this remote reservoir near the village of Tibi is formed by the oldest working dam in Europe.

 **Parque Municipal, Elx (Elche)**
MAP D6, Q1
This delightful palm-shaded park with tiled benches is right in the heart of town. The children's play areas make it perfect for family picnics.

7 Castillo de la Mola, Novelda
MAP D5
Squeezed up against a Modernista sanctuary, this lofty castle *(see p45)* offers far-reaching views across plains and a lunar landscape of jutting peaks.

8 Faro de Santa Pola
MAP E6, Q1
Santa Pola's lighthouse, at the tip of the cape, is a wonderful place to come at dusk, with views out across the cliffs to the tiny island of Tabarca.

9 Parque San Cayetano, Sierra de Crevillent
MAP C6
Whether you wish to arrive by car and leisurely enjoy the mountainous views, or hike to the 815-m (2,674-ft) peak of Monte San Cayetano, this picnic area by the Hermitage of San Cayetano is a great place to stop off.

10 El Palmeral, Orihuela
MAP P2
After a busy morning's sightseeing around Orihuela *(see p90)*, the charming and extensive palm grove on the edge of town makes a refreshing change and is perfect for picnics.

Spectacular scenery at Tibi reservoir

Alicante (Alacant) Shops

Colourful market stalls along the Explanada

1 Explanada Street Market

Canopied white stalls line Alicante's famous palm-lined promenade (see p16), with jewellery, ceramics, beachwear and more besides all on sale. Many stalls open during the day, but the market is liveliest on summer evenings.

2 Desigual

MAP T3 ■ Avda de Maisonnave 28–30 ■ 965 12 09 87

Desigual is one of Spain's most original designer brands. It offers various kinds of apparel for men, women and children, as well as homewares, all in colourful styles.

3 Pikolinos

MAP T3 ■ Avda Federico Soto 5 ■ 965 14 22 94

Founded in 1984, Pikolinos features mid-range, quality leather shoes, as well as leather bags and other accessories, which are all hand-crafted in Spain.

4 FNAC

MAP S3 ■ Avda de la Estación 5–7 ■ 687 635 088

At this popular book, music and electronic gadget superstore, you can sit undisturbed in a quiet corner and read one of the latest bestsellers, or listen to one of the many CDs they have on offer.

5 Ceramica Popular V. Pascual

MAP U2 ■ Avda Alfonso X El Sabio, 15 ■ 965 14 01 39

In business for over 120 years, this ceramics shop has colourful handmade pottery and tiles, along with a selection of herbs.

6 Turrones Espí

MAP U2 ■ C/Tomás López Torregrosa 17 ■ 965 21 44 41

Espí, one of the best *turrón* producers from Xixona (Jijona), has a small, exclusive shop in Alicante where you can buy their products.

7 Bodega Bernardino

MAP E5 ■ C/Alberola 40 ■ 965 28 08 73

Choose from over 2,500 wines, including an excellent regional Spanish selection, as well as wines from France, Chile and Argentina.

8 Adolfo Dominguez

MAP S3 ■ Avda Maisonave 53 ■ 608 79 81 77

Spanish designer Adolfo Dominguez offers an exclusive range of designer clothes for men and women.

9 Mercado Central

MAP T2 ■ Avda Alfonso X El Sabio

This delightful Modernista market is surrounded by colourful stalls selling fresh flowers. Inside, you'll find fabulous heaps of fruit, vegetables, fish and meat. Great for picnic supplies.

10 La Murciana

MAP T2 ■ Avda Alfonso X El Sabio 34 ■ 965 14 54 88

Widely regarded as the best *pastelería* in Alicante, La Murciana makes cakes, tarts and other sweet treats. Perfect to round off a gourmet picnic.

Alicante (Alacant) Tapas Bars

1 Nou Manolín

MAP U2 ■ C/Villegas 3 ■ 965 61 64 25 ■ Restaurant: €€€; tapas bar: €

Upstairs at Nou Manolín is one of the finest restaurants in Alicante *(see p97)*. Downstairs at the bar, the exceptional range and quality of the tapas means there's usually standing room only.

2 La Taberna del Gourmet

MAP T3 ■ C/San Fernando 10 ■ 965 20 42 33 ■ €€

This atmospheric little tapas bar is permanently packed. It serves a fine array of fresh tapas, and has an excellent wine list to accompany them, which includes some good local wines. The same owners also run the Terraza del Gourmet, on nearby Explanada.

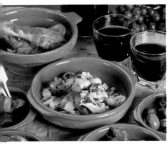

Selection of tapas

3 Restaurante Ibéricos

MAP U3 ■ C/Gerona 5 ■ 965 12 54 64 ■ Closed Sun ■ €€

The dangling hams signal this restaurant's speciality. A whole section of the menu is dedicated to ham, but there are plenty of other tasty dishes to choose from.

4 Cerveceria Sento

MAP U3 ■ C/Girona 1 ■ 646 93 22 13 ■ €

This diminutive bar serves what are said to be the best *montaditos* (sandwiches) in the whole city. There is another branch next to the cathedral, on Calle San Pascual.

PRICE CATEGORIES

For a three-course meal for one with half a bottle of wine (or equivalent meal), taxes and extra charges.

€ under €30 €€ €30–50 €€€ over €50

5 Bar Manero

MAP U3 ■ C/Manero Mollá 7 ■ 965 14 44 44 ■ www.barmanero.es ■ €

Styled like the late 19th century European bars, this place serves traditional Spanish tapas and has a huge wine selection.

6 Pinetell Tapas

MAP T2 ■ Carrer Navas 21 ■ 601 42 60 11 ■ €€

Centrally located, this cosy spot, with an outside terrace, specializes in ham croquets and rice dishes.

7 D´Tablas Alicante

MAP U3 ■ C/Rafael Altamira 6 ■ 966 61 11 14 ■ €

Although this venue can be a bit loud, it's worth it for the unbeatable prices. Friendly waiters circulate with trays of tapas for you to choose from.

8 Buen Comer

MAP U2 ■ C/Mayor 8 ■ 965 21 31 03 ■ www.elbuencomer.es ■ €€

This café-bar in the old quarter serves good tapas and *raciones* downstairs; upstairs, there's a fancier restaurant, with delicious seafood and rice dishes.

9 La Barra de César Anca

MAP U3 ■ C/Ojeda 1 ■ 965 12 43 62 ■ Closed Sun & Mon L ■ €€

A smart, modern tapas bar serving creative dishes that can be paired with the great wine selection.

10 Taberna Ibèrica

MAP U2 ■ C/Pedro Sebastiá 7 ■ 965 21 62 58 ■ Closed Sun & Mon D ■ €

Tucked away in the Old Town, this restaurant serves a range of typical regional dishes and delicious tapas.

See maps on p88–9

Nightlife

1 Clan Cabaret, Alicante (Alacant)
MAP T2 ■ C/Capitán Segarra 16 ■ 965 21 00 03 ■ www.clancabaret.com

With live music and drama, poetry readings and art exhibitions, this is a great place to relax. In summer, it converts into a disco every night.

2 Artespiritu, Alicante
MAP U2 ■ Plaza San Cristóbal 28 ■ 640 54 53 18

A trendy bar, Artespiritu specializes in mojitos and caipirinhas. It features DJs and live gigs at weekends.

3 Nic, Alicante
MAP U2 ■ C/Castaños 22 ■ 965 21 63 20

An elegant cocktail bar right in the city centre, Nic is the perfect place to start your evening.

4 Sala Stereo, Alicante
MAP U3 ■ C/Pintor Velázquez 5 ■ 965 20 49 57 ■ www.salastereo.com

A popular club and live music venue, Sala Stereo is known for its inclusion of rock and indie music to the regular mix of pop and electronica.

5 Frontera, Alicante
MAP E5 ■ Avda Costa Blanca 140, Playa de San Juan ■ 965 16 53 35

Located in the beachfront suburb of San Juan, this classic rock bar has been going strong since 1999 *(see p64)*.

6 C Breeze Lounge Bar, Torrevieja
MAP Q3 ■ CC Flamenca Beach 22 ■ 965 32 51 05

Friendly staff serve wonderful cocktails and cava at this bar.

7 De La Ville, Elx (Elche)
MAP D6 ■ C/Alfonso XIII 14 ■ www.delaville.es

This big disco pub in Elx has a giant screen showing sports events, and regular DJs. It often hosts big parties.

8 Camelot, Santa Pola
MAP E6, Q1 ■ Gran Playa ■ www.clubcamelot.es

This beachside club has an outdoor dance area. Spanish pop is interspersed with house and techno.

9 Artería, Elx
MAP D6 ■ C/Forn Fondo 1

A relaxed café-bar, Artería hosts art exhibitions, readings and other performances. Leaf through their books or relax outside on the terrace.

10 Casino Mediterraneo, Alicante
MAP V3 ■ Marina Deportiva, Muelle de Levante ■ 902 33 21 41

Offering slot machines, plus Black Jack, roulette and poker, this modern casino is on the outskirts of town.

Entrance to Casino Mediterraneo

Places to Eat

PRICE CATEGORIES

For a three-course meal for one with half a bottle of wine (or equivalent meal), taxes and extra charges.

€ under €30 €€ €30–50 €€€ over €50

Restaurante Gloria

MAP E6 ▪ C/Playa Tabarca s/n 03138, Isla Tabarca ▪ 965 96 03 78 ▪ €€

Enjoy lovely views of the beach while digging into generous rice dishes from a varied selection, including *arroz con bogavante* (rice with lobster).

2 Nou Manolín, Alicante (Alacant)

Excellent rice dishes, including *arroz a banda* (rice cooked in fish stock) are on offer at this welcoming restaurant with an elegant dining room upstairs and a superb tapas bar downstairs *(see p95)*.

Traditional Spanish dish
arroz a banda

3 Batiste, Santa Pola

MAP E6, Q1 ▪ Avda Fernando Pérez Ojeda 6 ▪ 965 41 14 85 ▪ €€

Traditional Valencian dishes of fresh fish, seafood and rice are the specialities at this restaurant.

4 Govana, Alicante

MAP E5 ▪ Plaza Doctor Gómez Ulla 4 ▪ 965 21 82 50 ▪ Closed Mon ▪ €€

Opposite the archaeological museum, this restaurant serves rice, local seafood and red meats from Galicia.

5 El Misteri d'Anna, Elx (Elche)

MAP D6 ▪ Avda Peña de las Aguilas ▪ 966 67 56 44 ▪ Closed Mon & Sun–Thu D ▪ €€

Diners have a choice of three dining rooms in which to enjoy dishes made with fresh seasonal produce.

6 Casablanca, Guardamar del Segura

Avda del Peru 2 ▪ MAP Q2 ▪ 966 72 58 22 ▪ Closed Jan ▪ €

This friendly, family-run restaurant located on the seafront serves breakfast, brunch, tapas, fresh seafood, steaks and more.

7 Piripi, Alicante

MAP S3 ▪ C/Óscar Esplá 30 ▪ 965 22 79 40 ▪ €€

One of Alicante's finest restaurants, this is a great option if you want to sample some of the local rice dishes in a welcoming ambience.

8 La Finca, Elx

MAP D6 ▪ Partida Perleta 1–7 ▪ 965 45 60 07 ▪ Closed Sun D; Mon; last 2 weeks Jan; Easter; Jun–Sep: Sun; 1 week Nov ▪ €€€

At La Finca in historic Elx, you are invited to "build your own menu". Chef Susi Díaz's playful sense of creativity is evident in her superb, innovative cuisine.

9 Nou Cucuch, Novelda

MAP D5 ▪ C/Argentina 18 ▪ 965 60 30 34 ▪ Closed Mon & Sun D ▪ €€

A traditional Spanish restaurant and tapas bar, Nou Cucuch is one of the best restaurants in Novelda. Here you can feast on a variety of classic local dishes prepared with a creative and sophisticated twist.

10 Xiri, Monóvar

MAP D5 ▪ Passeig de les Moreres 15 ▪ 965 47 29 10 ▪ Closed Mon & Tue; Wed & Sun D; 2 weeks Jul ▪ €€

Set in a lush park, this stylish, friendly restaurant offers diners refined Mediterranean cuisine. Remember to save room for one of the spectacular desserts.

See maps on pp88–9 →

TOP10 Costa Cálida

The sun shines, on average, for 300 days of the year on Murcia's "Warm Coast", which stretches from Europe's largest saltwater lagoon, the Mar Menor, down to the wild and rocky coastline around Águilas. If you're a watersports enthusiast, look no further than La Manga. But venture further south and you'll find the Parque Regional de Calblanque, one of the most beautiful stretches of coastline on the Mediterranean; the spectacular scenery of the Cabo Tiñoso; and Cartagena, the region's largest city, where Roman and Carthaginian ruins rub shoulders with Modernista mansions.

The imposing lighthouse at Cabo de Palos

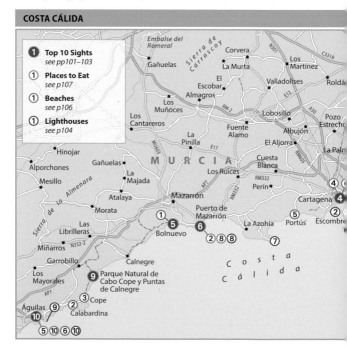

COSTA CÁLIDA

- **1** Top 10 Sights
  see pp101–103
- **1** Places to Eat
  see p107
- **1** Beaches
  see p106
- **1** Lighthouses
  see p104

Previous pages The wild beauty of Calblanque beach

1 Cabo de Palos
MAP Q5

Inhabited since Roman times, Cabo de Palos sits at the southernmost tip of the long spit separating the Mar Menor from the Mediterranean. A lighthouse offers amazing views of both seas and the coastline. The village retains its fishing tradition, and you'll find good seafood restaurants here, but the star attraction is the proximity of the beautiful Calblanque regional park (see pp12–13).

2 Santiago de la Ribera
MAP P4

This modern resort on the shores of the Mar Menor offers an excellent marina and a long, palm-lined prom-enade. This was once a humble fishing village, and a few colourful boats remain. The tranquil waters here are ideal for anyone learning to sail or windsurf, and there are excel-lent facilities for watersports. Ferries regularly sail for Isla Perdiguera.

The shallow waters of the Mar Menor

3 Mar Menor
MAP P4

Europe's largest saltwater lagoon, the Mar Menor has over 70 km (43 miles) of coastline. Relatively shallow, with a maximum depth of 7 m (23 ft), it is always several degrees warmer than the Mediterranean, and its high salt content makes it easier to float in. The sea is strewn with volcanic islands: Isla Barón is the largest, but pretty Isla Perdiguera is most visited.

4 Cartagena
MAP P5

Founded by the Carthaginians in the 3rd century BC, resettled by the Romans, and beloved by the Arabs, Cartagena has had a long, dramatic history. The old town features fine Roman ruins and is overlooked by a castle. The Calle Mayor is still lined with flamboyant Modernista mansions and the city's naval history is told in the fascinating Museo Nacional de Arqueología Subacuática (see p102).

Cartagena's Roman amphitheatre

5 Ciudad Encantada de Bolnuevo
MAP M5

The little fishing village and tourist resort of Bolnuevo has a fine, dark sandy beach and a series of beautiful coves to its south, reached by a winding road, which hugs the cliff. These coves are well off the beaten track, so they are popular with naturists. Behind the main beach is the Ciudad Encantada, an "enchanted city" of bizarre rock formations eroded by the wind and sea into extraordinary shapes *(see p54)*.

> **WORLD'S FIRST MILITARY SUB**
>
> The Naval Museum in Cartagena has on display what is claimed to be the first operational military submarine in the world. Launched in 1888, the vessel was powered by an electric battery and equipped with a torpedo tube. It was invented by naval officer, designer and engineer Isaac Peral (1851–95), who was born in Cartagena.

monuments, including the Modernista town hall and the pretty 16th-century church of San Andrés.

Marina at Puerto de Mazarrón

6 Puerto de Mazarrón
MAP M5

The modest resort of Puerto de Mazarrón, one of the most southerly on the Costa Cálida, is popular with Murcian families. An attractive fishing port and marina sit next to each other at the foot of a jutting cape; around it spread low-key developments and long beaches of dark sand interspersed with rocky coves. The resort is linked to the neighbouring village of Mazarrón, with a smattering of historic

7 La Manga del Mar Menor
MAP Q4

La Manga – "The Sleeve" – is the name given to the curious, long spit of land that divides the Mar Menor from the Mediterranean. The entire 21 km (13 miles) length is now packed with a virtually unbroken line of high-rise apartment buildings and hotels, which is visible for miles around. Dedicated entirely to summer fun, the beaches are lined with bars, cafés and restaurants, and offer numerous opportunities for watersports, including windsurfing, water-skiing, fishing and sailing. Regular ferries ply between La Manga and the islands of the Mar Menor.

8 Calblanque

One of the most beautiful stretches of coastline in the region, the Calblanque has crystal-clear waters that are perfect for snorkelling and diving. Behind the shore lie pine-clad mountains, with excellent walking and mountain-biking trails *(see pp12–13)*.

Beach along Calblanque coastline

⑨ Parque Natural de Cabo Cope y Puntas de Calnegre

MAP L6

As you progress to the southernmost tip of Murcia's Costa Cálida, the terrain becomes increasingly wild and rocky. This hauntingly lovely cape is now a protected Natural Park, and home to all kinds of birds and animals, including wild boar, sea turtles, cormorants and peregrine falcons. Footpaths are traced through the scrub, and you can climb to the summit of the cape for stunning views of the sheer cliffs and the wheeling seabirds. In the lee of the cape is a dramatic stretch of rocky inlets and coves, perfect for a dip, overlooked by a 16th-century watchtower built to defend the coast from pirates.

Boats docked at the harbour, Águilas

⑩ Águilas

MAP L6

Nudged up against the border with Andalucía, this quiet resort curls around a broad sandy bay, with spectacular rocky capes at either end and a few volcanic islands rising abruptly from the sea. The delightful port sits at the foot of a steep cliff at the southern end of the bay; it's full of working fishing boats, which supply delicious fresh fish to the local restaurants. The Castle of San José, beautifully flood-lit at night, looms dramatically from the clifftop. In February, the town hosts one of the biggest carnivals in Spain (see p74).

A WALK AROUND CARTAGENA

▶ **MORNING**

This easy walk around the city centre of **Cartagena** (see p101) is a great way to spend a morning as it takes you on a journey back in time from the present day through Modernism to the Roman era.

Leaving the tourist information office, turn left (away from the sea) and go up to the Plaza del Ayuntamiento beneath the handsome façade of the city hall, the Palacio Consistorial. Continue in the same direction up Calle Mayor, which contains several fine Modernista buildings. The three finest are on the left: Casa Cervantes (with its white bay windows), the **Casino** (see p46) and Casa Llagostera, which has magnificent ceramic decorations.

At Plaza San Sebastian turn hard right round the corner formed by the old **Gran Hotel** (see p47) and wander down Calle Aire, passing the 18th-century church of Santa Maria de Gracia and the pretty pink-and-white façade of the Modernista mansion Casa Clares (on the corner of Calle Cuadro Santos). Calle Aire brings you to the stunning 1st-century BC excavated Teatro Romano. If you have the energy, take the steps up to the viewpoint in Parque Torres. Alternatively, **El Cantón** tapas bar (see p107) beside the theatre is the perfect place for a drink or lunch, where you can feast on a selection of seafood specialities.

To get back to your starting point set off back up Calle Aire and turn left down Calle Cañon.

See map on pp100–101

Lighthouses

 1 La Manga
MAP Q5

Almost at the tip of "the sleeve" (La Manga), this enormous lighthouse sits above the biggest marina on the Mar Menor, and looks out over the Mediterranean and a pair of miniature islands.

2 Cartagena
One of the biggest ports in Spain, Cartagena is spread around a huge natural bay (see p101). Its sturdy red-brick lighthouse keeps watch over the endless flotillas of container ships coming in to dock.

 3 Islas Hormigas
MAP Q5

These tiny, rocky islets off Cabo de Palos are topped by another lighthouse – a beautiful sight at dusk.

 4 Punta Negra
MAP P5

Perched over a tiny bay with unusual dark sand, this lighthouse stands at the western end of the beautiful Parque Regional de Calblanque (see pp12–13). Walking trails splinter off in all directions, and there's a spectacular hike along the cliffs.

 5 Cabo de Palos
The view from the huge lighthouse overlooking the fishing village of Cabo de Palos (see p101) is very different depending on which way you face: on one side, you'll see the Mediterranean crashing dramatically on the cliffs; on the other are the tranquil waters of the Mar Menor.

 6 Islas de Escombreras
MAP P5

A few islets are strewn around the entrance to the enormous port at Cartagena; a lighthouse, visible from the cape below Escombreras, gives early warning to ships.

 7 Cabo Tiñoso
MAP N5

A straggling dirt track leads to the lighthouse at the tip of this wild and beautiful headland, gazing out over crashing waves, long fingers of rock, and tiny hidden bays.

 8 Puerto de Mazarrón
The family resort of Puerto de Mazarrón is sprawled around a cove-studded cape (see p102). A dusty path wriggles to the top for beautiful sea views from the lighthouse.

9 Punta del Poniente
MAP L6

The coastline gets wilder as it heads down the Costa Cálida. The lighthouse at the tip of the Punta del Poniente (north of Águilas) keeps watch over sheer cliffs and scores of tiny islands.

10 Águilas
The lighthouse of Águilas stands guard at the southern end of the bay, near the town's pretty fishing port (see p103). Painted in black and white stripes, it looks like something out of a storybook. To complete the picture, above it looms the dramatic castle.

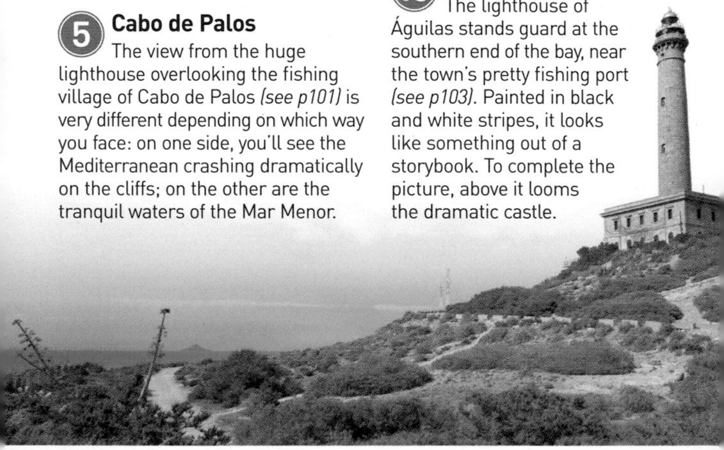

Lighthouse on the Cabo de Palos peninsula

Sports Facilities

Windsurfing on the Mediterranean

1 Windsurfing
■ www.escuelasandrina.com

Sailboards for windsurfing can be hired at almost every beach on the Mar Menor. The quiet inland sea is good for beginners; more advanced windsurfers can try the Mediterranean.

2 Diving
■ www.zoeaaguilas.es

Most of the resorts on the Mar Menor and the southern resorts of Puerto de Mazarrón and Águilas have companies offering diving courses, excursions and equipment hire.

3 Sailing
■ www.pro-vela.com

The Mar Menor is famous for its many marinas and fine sailing facilities. The tranquil inland sea is ideal for beginners, and there is plenty to keep experienced sailors happy on the Mediterranean side of La Manga.

4 Tennis

Many large hotels around the Mar Menor have tennis courts, and usually let non-residents play for a fee. Most larger towns along the coast have municipal courts, which can be hired through the tourist office.

5 Fishing

Fishing is popular, but requires permits. Find information at tourist offices or local fishing-tackle shops.

6 Bird-watching

The salt lakes in the Parque Regional de Calblanque (see pp12–13) attract numerous birds, as do the salt flats around Lo Pagán, on the northern shores of the Mar Menor.

7 Horse Riding
■ www.centroecuestresoto mayor.es

There are several stables around the Mar Menor, including in Santa Ana, that offer treks around Calblanque.

8 Hiking

The Parque Natural de Cabo Cope y Puntas de Calnegre has good hiking, but the best trails can be found in the Parque Regional de Calblanque. The GR92 walking path runs the length of the Costa Cálida.

9 Golf
■ www.lamangaclub.com; www.golfaltorreal.es

La Manga Club and Altorreal Golf have championship courses, which are open to all on payment of green fees.

Golf course at La Manga Club

10 Snorkelling

The coast's many coves are perfect for snorkelling, but the best is the Parque Regional de Calblanque, with clear waters and secluded bays. Get your own gear or rent elsewhere.

See map on pp100–101

Beaches

Long expanse of golden sand at Bolnuevo beach

 Bolnuevo
This resort's long, sandy beach (see p102) is backed by some incredibly surreal rock formations (see p54), and has plenty of cafés and other facilities. To really get away from it all, head south down the coast to dozens of secret coves.

 Calabardina
MAP L6
Tucked around a tiny bay, pretty little Calabardina is a charming and barely developed resort, featuring several quiet beaches and rocky coves.

 Fuente de Cope
MAP L6
Near the watchtower in the Parque Natural de Cabo Cope y Puntas de Calnegre (see p103), this is an unspoiled stretch of coastline, with rocky outcrops and pools sheltered by the impressive cape.

4 **Calblanque**
The beaches of the Parque Regional de Calblanque are the best in the whole of the Costa Cálida. Choose from long stretches of golden sand, or discover your own private cove (see pp12–13).

5 **Portús**
MAP N5
Tucked in the lee of a rocky headland south of Cartagena, this narrow pebbly beach is well off the beaten track. There are little bays to be discovered, and it's an authorized nudist beach.

6 **Águilas**
The elegant curve of Águilas's bay is broken by strangely shaped volcanic islands, which are perfect for snorkelling. Long, fine sands and plenty of amenities make it highly popular with families (see p103).

7 **Punta Negra**
Escape the crowds in this tiny cove (see p104) near the ghostly former mining town of Portmán. The shingled beaches are dotted with upturned boats. Nearby, there's excellent walking in the Regional Park of Calblanque.

8 **Playa Honda**
MAP Q5
One of the most popular beaches on the Mar Menor, the Playa Honda is a wonderful 7-km (4-mile) stretch of sand around Mar de Cristal, with every imaginable facility.

9 **Santiago de la Ribera**
The main beach of this upmarket resort (see p101) is backed by a wooden, palm-shaded boardwalk, and the long sandy expanse is lined with countless bars and cafés. It's particularly good for families.

10 **Cala del Pino**
MAP Q4
On the Mar Menor side of La Manga, this popular beach with fine sand looks out over the islets dotting the inland sea. Many facilities (including a marina) are close at hand.

Places to Eat

1 MardeSal, San Pedro del Pinatar

MAP P3 ■ Playa de la Llana ■ 650 16 45 92 ■ Closed Oct–mid-Jun: Sun–Thu D ■ €€

Enjoy salads, seafood, meat and rice dishes. The highlight is *caldreta de bogavante* (lobster and seafood stew).

2 El Puerto, Puerto de Mazarrón

MAP M5 ■ Plaza del Mar ■ 968 59 48 05 ■ Closed Tue ■ €€

Right on the port, El Puerto specializes in seafood. The *caldereta de langosta* (prawn stew) is wonderful.

3 El Mosqui, Cabo de Palos

MAP Q5 ■ Subida al Faro 50 ■ 68 56 45 63 ■ Closed L & Tue in winter ■ €

Enjoy excellent *caldero* (stew) as well as a fresh *pescado frito* (fried fish platter) at this spot with a nautical feel.

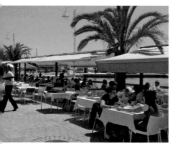

Harbourfront dining, Cabo de Palos

4 Restaurante d'Almansa, Cartagena

MAP P5 ■ C/Jabonerías 53 ■ 868 09 96 66 ■ Closed 2 weeks Jun ■ €€

This elegant restaurant serves a range of interesting tasting menus as well as à la carte offerings.

5 El Pimiento, Águilas

MAP L6 ■ C/Don Joaquín Tendero 1 ■ 968 44 87 23 ■ Closed L ■ €

One of the most popular tapas bars in town, El Pimiento's menu is very traditional. Dishes include potatoes with garlic, *michirones* (a bean-and-sausage stew), and delicious hams.

PRICE CATEGORIES

For a three-course meal for one with half a bottle of wine (or equivalent meal), taxes and extra charges.

€ under €30 **€€** €30–50 **€€€** over €50

6 El Cantón, Cartagena

MAP P5 ■ Cuesta de la Baronesa 1 ■ 630 85 17 43 ■ €

Located next to the Roman Theatre, this is a traditional tapas-bar. The menu offers seafood specialities and anchovies on toast.

7 Restaurante La Tana, Cabo de Palos

MAP Q5 ■ Calle del Faro 2 ■ 968 56 30 03 ■ Closed Dec ■ €€

Good seafood and rice dishes include the house speciality *arroz la Tana*, a succulent stew of squid and shrimp.

8 Viggos, Puerto de Mazarrón

MAP M5 ■ Paseo de la Sal 1 ■ 968 15 45 44 ■ ■ Closed Tue ■ €

This seafront spot is great if you want an inexpensive meal with a wide range of options. The menu features platters of fried fish, pizza and pasta.

9 Restaurante Juan Mari

MAP P3 ■ Avda Emilio Castelar 113 ■ 968 18 62 98 ■ Closed Sun & Mon D, Tue ■ €€

Relish exquisitely prepared seasonal dishes, including fish and rice options, all made with local produce at this family-run place.

10 El Faro, Águilas

MAP L6 ■ C/José María Pereda s/n ■ 968 41 28 83 ■ Closed Wed ■ €€

Popular with a younger crowd, El Faro serves tasty local dishes on the seafront at reasonable prices.

See map on pp100–101

TOP10 Inland Murcia

Murcia is Spain at its most traditional and unspoiled. Enchanting villages spill down hillsides topped with ruined castles, and verdant fields and orchards recall the Arabs who first cultivated these lands. The Romans brought vines to the region, and wine is still made in the charming wine towns of Jumilla, Bullas and Yecla. Wild sierras fan out to the furthest corners of the province; the loveliest of them all is the Parque Regional de Sierra Espuña, a forested mountain range, scattered with ancient snow wells, and home to a wonderful variety of animal and bird life. Murcia City bursts with Baroque churches and palaces, and its sumptuous cathedral is one of the finest in Spain.

Catedral de Santa María, Murcia

1 Murcia City
MAP N3

The capital city of Murcia Province is a delightful mix of old and new, with flamboyant Baroque churches – including the magnificent Catedral de Santa María *(see pp34–5)* – elegant modern shopping avenues, fragrant public gardens and intriguing muse-ums all clustered together in the old centre. The graceful squares are full of excellent tapas bars and restaurants.

INLAND MURCIA

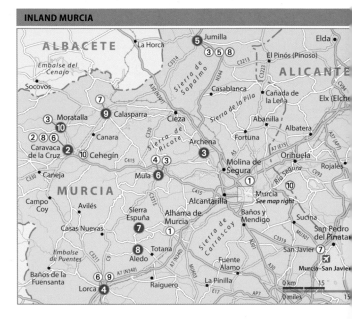

Castle overlooking the hilltop town of Caravaca de la Cruz

② Caravaca de la Cruz
MAP K2

Pretty Caravaca de la Cruz *(see p45)*, set among the sierras of northeastern Murcia, is dominated by its handsome castle, built by the Knights Templar after the Reconquest. This contains Caravaca's greatest treasure, the Santuario de la Vera Cruz, which holds a relic of the True Cross, brought here, according to legend, by two angels in 1231. The miracle is celebrated annually on 2 May, when the relic is paraded through the streets.

③ Archena
MAP M2

There is little to see in the sleepy market town of Archena besides the Baroque Church of San Juan Bautista and a few neglected mansions, but its spa (Balneario de Archena) has been famous since Roman times. Prettily located on the banks of the River Segura, the spa is now a miniature village, with a delightful chapel and a 19th-century casino. There are three hotels, and a whole range of health and beauty treatments on offer.

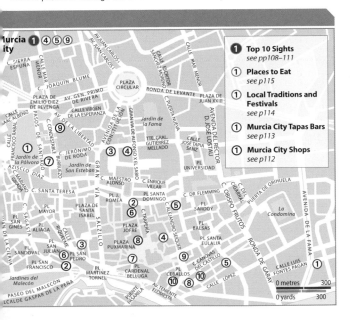

Murcia City

① **Top 10 Sights**
  see pp108–111

① **Places to Eat**
  see p115

① **Local Traditions and Festivals**
  see p114

① **Murcia City Tapas Bars**
  see p113

① **Murcia City Shops**
  see p112

Ex-Colegiata de San Patricio, Lorca

4 Lorca
MAP K4

An elegant, historic city sprawling beneath the ruins of a 13th-century fortress, Lorca is celebrated today for its wealth of Baroque architecture and lavish Easter Week processions. The beautiful Plaza de España, at the heart of the old quarter is overlooked by the arcaded 17th-century town hall and the splendid Ex-Colegiata de San Patricio *(see p42)*. The way to the castle, known as the Fortress of the Sun, leads past another church, the Iglesia de Santa María. For a good view of the castle, climb the 1,321 steps of the Via Crucis from Calle de Nogalte to the San Clemente hermitage, passing the stations of the cross.

5 Jumilla
MAP A4

Jumilla, an unassuming town piled chaotically on a hillside, is surrounded by vines *(see p52)*. The Romans first introduced wine to the area almost 2,000 years ago, and it's been made here ever since. Find out about its history in the local Museo del Vino, or take a tour of the *bodegas* for a taste of what's on offer. The old town has a pair of pretty churches and is crowned by a 15th-century castle, which offers fine views of the vine-covered plain and distant sierras.

6 Mula
MAP L2

The town of Mula clings to a steep hillside beneath the impressive ruins of a 16th-century castle. The intricate maze of winding streets at the heart of the old quarter recalls the town's Arabic origins. Here are faded mansions and elaborate churches. On the fringes of the town, the delightful spa at Baños de Mula has been famous since Roman times.

7 Sierra Espuña

A nature-rich area of wooded inland mountains forms the heart of this stunning reserve *(see pp26–7)* which is a good place for hiking, botanising and bird-watching.

8 Aledo
MAP L4

The peaceful medieval village of Aledo is huddled tightly behind vestiges of ancient walls, on a rocky outcrop that juts out over the surrounding valley. At the edge of the village is a watchtower, surrounded by a modern walkway that offers fine views over the terraced hillsides and distant peaks. Just 3 km (2 miles) away, an 18th-century sanctuary houses a much-venerated image of the local patron saint, Santa Eulalia. Aledo also sits right on the borders of the wonderful Parque Regional de Sierra Espuña.

Wild boar, Sierra de Espuña

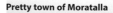

Pretty town of Moratalla

LA VIRGEN DE LA ESPERANZA

A shepherd discovered the "Virgin of Hope" in a cave near Calasparra, but the tiny statue miraculously grew too heavy to lift when the townspeople came to transfer it to a church. The sanctuary they built over the cave has been the focus of popular pilgrimages ever since, and the Virgin remains one of the most venerated in Spain.

9 Calasparra
MAP K1

Calasparra overlooks a lush valley on the banks of the River Segura. During the Middle Ages, it was a key frontier settlement controlled by the Order of the Knights of Malta, who built its 13th-century castle. Now, it's an agricultural town surrounded by a sea of blossom in spring, and golden rice fields in the autumn. Rice features prominently on local menus *(see p64)*.

10 Moratalla
MAP K1

Medieval Moratalla is a tawny huddle of stone houses piled around a sturdy castle. A traditional mountain town with few monuments, its charm lies in its beautiful surroundings and quiet pace of life. Festivals, particularly Easter Week, are celebrated in old-fashioned style. On Maundy Thursday, Good Friday and Easter Sunday, the town resounds to the sound of almost a thousand drummers marching through the centre of town.

A DAY IN INLAND MURCIA

▶ MORNING

Allow a full day for this drive, which includes time for hiking. Begin at the little mountain village of **Aledo**, with panoramic views of peaks and valleys, before following the signs for Bullas and turning off at the **Sierra Espuña**. Continue along the twisting mountain road, which offers breathtaking glimpses of forested crags. The left-hand turn signposted *pozos de nieve* will take you to the ancient snow wells, reached by a path from a small car park at the crook of the road. This is a great place for a hike and a picnic. Return to the Collado Bermejo and take the right-hand fork through forests and glades of wild flowers to the Visitor Information Centre and exhibition. Have lunch at the nearby Fuente del Hilo *(Carretera de España; 968 43 92 23)*, closed Aug, where wild boar snuffle fearlessly at the doorway for dropped crumbs.

AFTERNOON

After lunch, take the signposted road for the little hamlet of El Berro, which lies close to the arid wilderness of the **Barrancos de Gebas** *(see p27)*, otherwise known as the "bad lands". There are some lovely panoramic views from the Caserío de Gebas on the C3315. The road leads north to Pliego, a sleepy village topped with a ruined tower, and on to **Mula** *(see p44)*, with its fascinating medieval centre and striking ruined castle. Enjoy a tasty dinner at the **Gastrobar El Casino** *(see p115)*.

See map on pp108–109 ←

Murcia City Shops

1 El Centro de Artesanía

MAP S4 ■ C/Francisco Rabal 8
■ 968 35 75 37

The best place to find Murcian arts and crafts, from ceramics to hand-made figurines, is run by the provincial government. There are two other branches in Lorca and Cartagena.

Mercado de las Verónicas, Murcia

2 Mercado de las Verónicas
MAP T6 ■ Plano de San Francisco

Set in a Modernista building, Murcia's delightful covered market offers a huge variety of fresh produce, including fish and locally reared meats.

3 Confitería Carlos
MAP T4 ■ C/Jaime I El Conquistador 7 ■ 968 23 30 20 ■ Closed Aug

The Arabs introduced the delicious pastries for which Murcia is still celebrated. The tempting selection in this cake shop includes *paparajotes* (light, lemon-flavoured pastries).

4 Zenia Boutique
MAP U4 ■ C/Jaime I el Conquistador 3 ■ 968 22 34 74

A range of chic clothing, including Spanish and international designers, is offered at this boutique.

5 Enoteca Selección Casa Rambla
MAP U5 ■ C/Saavedra Fajardo 15
■ 968 21 67 64

This enormous shop sells a huge selection of local, Spanish and international wines, along with a range of liqueurs and fiery local spirits.

6 The Room Shops
MAP U5 ■ C/Gonzalez Adalid 13 ■ 868 05 27 19 ■ www.theroom shops.com

Everything from fashion items to a range of unusual crafts are sold at this little souvenir shop close to Murcia's biggest sight, the Baroque cathedral (see pp34–5).

7 Calzados Luz
MAP T4 ■ C/Jerónimo de Roda 1 ■ 968 28 42 49

Mostly Spanish high-quality leather shoes for men and women can be found at this stylish shoe shop.

8 Nuut Gourmet - La Fonda Negra
MAP U5 ■ C/González Adalid 1 ■ 968 88 43 04 ■ www.nuutgourmet.com

A gourmet and gift shop, this place sells all kinds of delicious Spanish produce. The shelves are stocked with oils, wines, different types of cheese, hams and a Spanish favourite: conserved seafood.

9 Sasasú Handmade
MAP T4 ■ Plaza Condestable 5 ■ 678 18 68 05

This boutique attached to a workshop features unique bags made by hand in leather or *polipiel* (faux leather) by local artists.

10 Pasteleria Baklava
MAP U6 ■ C/Ceballos, 5 ■ 632 26 88 31 ■ Open 6–11pm Mon–Sat ■ www.pasteleriabaklava.com

Situated by the university, this pastry shop serves good tea and coffee. The aromatic infusions sit alongside spectacular traditional Arab sweets.

➤ See maps on pp108–109

Murcia City Tapas Bars

PRICE CATEGORIES

For a three-course meal for one with half a bottle of wine (or equivalent meal), taxes and extra charges.

€ under €30 €€ €30–50 €€€ over €50

① Bodega El Jumilano

MAP N3 ▪ C/Luís Fontes Pagán 6 ▪ 968 34 55 17 ▪ €

Choose from a mix of traditional and modern dishes at this tavern, which also features art exhibitions.

② Café del Arco

MAP U5 ▪ C/Arco de Santo Domingo s/n ▪ 628 11 15 73 ▪ €

This elegant café-bar has a huge terrace on a graceful square and is perfect for a leisurely breakfast or lunch and for people-watching.

③ La Tapa

MAP T5 ▪ Plaza de las Flores 13 ▪ 968 21 13 17 ▪ €

A simple, buzzy tapas bar on one of Murcia's liveliest squares. Sit out on the terrace to watch the action.

④ Keki de Sergio Martínez

MAP U5 ▪ Calle Funesanta 4 ▪ 968 22 07 98 ▪ Closed Mon ▪ €€

A stylish restaurant that serves complete lunch at a reasonable price. In the evening the chef will serve you 8 or 10 tapas of his choice.

⑤ El Girasol

MAP V5 ▪ Calle San Jose 22 ▪ 968 21 72 35 ▪ €

This vegetarian restaurant a few streets east of the cathedral uses mainly organic ingredients and offers a reasonably priced set menu at lunchtime. Vegan and gluten free options are available.

⑥ La Tapeoteca

MAP T6 ▪ Plaza San Pedro 3 ▪ 663 72 40 59 ▪ Closed Sun D ▪ €

A small, stylish tapas bar that also serves creative mains. Try the *ravioli de rabo de toro* (oxtail ravioli) or the *cucuruchos de salmón con helado de wasabi* (salmon cones with wasabi ice cream). Reservations recommended.

⑦ Los Zagales

MAP U6 ▪ C/Polo de Medina 4 ▪ 968 21 55 79 ▪ Closed Sun ▪ €

Just around the corner from the cathedral, this is a great place to enjoy a plate of tapas.

⑧ Taberna Típica La Pequeña

MAP U6 ▪ Plaza San Juan 8 ▪ 968 21 98 40 ▪ Closed Sun D in winter ▪ €€

The name says it all. A typical tavern serving Murcian specialities, with first-rate local cured sausages and hams.

⑨ Rincón de Pepe

MAP U6 ▪ C/Apóstoles 34 ▪ 610 99 99 99 ▪ €€€

The best-known restaurant in town specializes in exquisite Mediterranean cuisine.

⑩ Pura Cepa

MAP N3 ▪ Plaza del Rescate de Cristo ▪ 968 21 73 97 ▪ Closed Sun & Mon L ▪ €€

A range of tapas and traditional Murcian dishes with a modern twist are served here. Choose from the bar's fine selection of Spanish wines and enjoy the terrace in summer.

Murcian tapas bar

Local Traditions and Festivals

1 Carnavales
MAP N3

Carnival is an excuse to party across the region (see p74). One key location is to the north of Murcia city centre, in the Cabezo de Torres neighbourhood.

2 Semana Santa

Holy Week is huge, with lavish processions taking place all 7 days. The biggest are held in Murcia City, Cartagena, Jumilla, Lorca and Cieza.

3 Martes Santo
MAP L2 (Mula), K1 (Moratalla)

On Holy Tuesday, a loud parade of drummers marches through Mula during the Noche de los Tambores (see p44). There are other tamboradas at Moratalla on Maundy Thursday and Good Friday.

Good Friday Easter procession

4 Viernes Santo
MAP N3

Good Friday has a special significance in Murcia City. The week's processions culminate with a parade of gilded pasos (floats) that feature sculptures by the celebrated Baroque artist Francisco Salzillo.

5 Fiestas de Primavera
MAP N3

Murcia City's Spring Fiesta (from the Tuesday after Easter Sunday) begins with the Battle of the Flowers and the Bando de la Huerta, a parade of amusing satirical floats. A pagan ritual called the "Burial of the Sardine" marks the end of the fiesta.

6 Fiestas de la Cruz de Caravaca
MAP K2

In the first week of May, Caravaca (see p45) celebrates ancient legends and miracles with processions of "knights" on horseback and other traditional events during the Festivities of the Cross of Caravaca.

7 Festival Internacional de Teatro, Música y Danza
MAP N3

One of the biggest cultural events on the Murcian summer calendar, San Javier's International Festival of Theatre, Music and Dance is a great opportunity to see international performers at venues across the city.

8 Fiesta de la Vendimia
MAP A4

Jumilla celebrates its ancient Wine Harvest Festival each year in the last two weeks of August.

9 Murcia Tres Culturas
MAP N3

Taking place annually since 2000 in the city of Murcia throughout the month of May, this festival celebrates the historical union of Christian, Jewish and Muslim cultures, which have influenced Spain throughout the centuries. There are dance, music and theatre performances.

10 Matanza

As in times gone by, farming families in inland Murcian towns still slaughter their pigs every November to create the famous embutidos (cured sausages and hams) (see p66).

Places to Eat

El Chaleco, Alhama de Murcia

MAP M3 ■ Avenida Bastarreche 9
■ 968 63 01 04 ■ Closed Mon & Tue, Wed
& Sun D (Jul & Aug), 1st half Aug ■ €€

Traditional Murcian specialities,
including tasty desserts and regional
wines, are served at El Chaleco.

2 Rincón de Paco, Caravaca de la Cruz

MAP K2 ■ C/Lonja 5 ■ 968 70 83 90
■ Closed Tue ■ €

The bar of this popular restaurant is
lined with bull-related memorabilia.

3 Loreto, Jumilla

MAP A4 ■ C/de las Canalejas 73
■ 968 78 03 60 ■ Closed Mon, Sun–
Thu D & Jul ■ €€

Set in a townhouse, Loreto serves
regional cuisine with a creative twist,
and has a great wine list.

4 Gastrobar El Casino, Mula

MAP L2 ■ Plaza del Ayuntamiento
■ 627 92 20 13 ■ Closed Mon ■ €€

With two zones – the tapas bar and
dining room – this gastrobar caters
to all appetites. Both serve creative
and beautifully presented dishes.

5 Casa Sebastián, Jumilla

MAP A4 ■ Avda Levante 6
■ 968 78 01 94 ■ Closed D & Sun ■ €

Traditional cuisine is the highlight
of this simple, rustic restaurant. Try
the delicious Jumillano gazpacho.

6 Casa de los Musso, Lorca

MAP K4 ■ C/del Álamo 30
■ 628 61 18 72 ■ Closed Sun ■ €€

Located in an 18th-century building,
this family restaurant serves sophisticated Spanish cuisine prepared with
excellent local produce. Try the
barbecued meats.

7 Hospederia Rural Constitución, Calasparra

MAP K1 ■ Plaza de la Constitución 10
■ 968 72 08 01 ■ €

Next to the museum and the town's
church, this spot serves simple
traditional Murcian cuisine. It offers
a well-priced weekday menú del día
and a good choice of wines.

8 Fuentes del Marqués, Caravaca de la Cruz

MAP K2 ■ Paraje Fuentes del Marqués
■ 968 70 00 87 ■ €€

Tuck into hearty local dishes in this
country restaurant with lovely views.

9 Paredes, Lorca

MAP K4 ■ Carretera Granada
Km 588 ■ 626 27 77 25 ■ €€

A pleasing mixture of the traditional
and the contemporary influences both
the food and decor at this popular
restaurant. Fresh, locally
sourced produce is key to
the refined cuisine.

10 El Sol, Cehegín

MAP K2 ■ C/Mayor
17 ■ 968 74 00 64 ■ Closed
Mon (except summer), 1st
half Jul ■ €

Old-fashioned El Sol, in the
heart of medieval Cehegín,
serves traditional Murcian
dishes with a twist. You can
dine out on a little terrace.

Traditional presentation of gazpacho soup

See maps on pp108–109 ←

Streetsmart

A bustling promenade
in the Marina of Alicante

Getting Around

Arriving by Air

Alicante-Elche Airport is the region's main hub. It is connected to the UK and other European countries by many air-lines, including **Ryanair**, **easyJet** and **Jet2**.

Murcia-San Javier Airport is much smaller and receives fewer flights, handling only eight airlines. It is located beside the Mar Menor and is 50 km (30 miles) by road from Murcia city. There are no direct flights to either of these airports from North America. US and Canadian visitors must fly to Madrid, Málaga or Barcelona and pick up a domestic flight or a train. **Iberia**, Spain's flag-carrying airline, flies between several major cities in the US and Madrid. For all flights, book early in high season and check online for the best deals.

Arriving by Sea

Balearia operates the ferry route from Denia (Dénia) to the Balearic Islands, with calls at Formentera, Ibiza and Mallorca. **Algérie Ferries** connects Alicante with Oran, Mostaganem and Algiers in Algeria, North Africa.

International Train Travel

The French high-speed rail network (TGV) joins its Spanish counterpart on the border in the western Pyrenees to provide direct services from Paris to Barcelona. As London is linked to Paris by Eurostar

and Barcelona is linked to Alicante (Alacant) by the high-speed Euromed service, it is possible to get from the UK to the Costa Blanca in an average of 22 hours of travel. Inter-city trains in Spain are operated by **Renfe**. France's national rail company **SNCF** has details on international routes and sells tickets.

Long-Distance Bus Travel

Eurolines runs services from London and Paris to Valencia and **Alicante Coach Station**. Journey times can be longer than the train but ticket prices are much cheaper if you book ahead.

Buses

Many inland villages aren't on the train network, and are only accessible by bus. Different companies serve different areas. Information offices in bus stations, and tourist offices (see p123) have timetables.

Regional and Local Trains and Trams

Spain has a comparatively small rail network. Murcia and Alicante form part of Renfe's Levante region, which is structured around three main lines: Alicante to Valencia via Xativa (Játiva), Alicante to Murcia and Cartagena via Elx (Elche), and Alicante to Albacte via Villena.

Renfe Feve (a subsidiary of the mainline company) operates a narrow-gauge railway from Cartagena

to Los Nietos on the Mar Menor. Trains run hourly during the day and the journey takes 28 minutes.

The **Alicante Tram** system extends far to the north with Line 1 going from Alicante-Luceros station to Benidorm. From there, Line 9 reaches Denia via Calp (Calpe). The journey takes about 3 hours, and there are good views along some stretches.

Taxis

Taxis are plentiful in the larger towns and resorts. They can be hailed on the street or from taxi stands; a green light on the top of the vehicles indicates that they are free. Otherwise, you can call for a taxi. Reputable firms include **Taxi Alicante** and **Radio Taxi Murcia**.

Driving to Costa Blanca

The motorway down Spain's east coast, the AP7 (known as the E15), is the fastest way to reach Costa Blanca from France. Note that tolls can be quite expensive. The toll-free main road, N340, is much slower. The AP36 (toll) and AP31 connects Alicante with Madrid. Before leaving, ensure that your car is equipped with two warning triangles and a reflective jacket in case of a roadside emergency.

Driving the Costa Blanca

Your own transport is virtually essential to see the remoter corners of the

Costa Blanca but if you are going to stay mostly in one city or resort, which is likely to be clogged with traffic in peak periods, it is not worth the hassle.

There are car-hire offices at airports, train stations and in major towns and resorts. The cheapest deals can usually be found online before you travel; many airlines offer discounted car hire at the time of booking.

Road signs mostly conform to European standard and the obvious rules apply: the use of seat belts is compulsory and there are strict rules on drinking and driving, which are enforced through random checks and on-the-spot fines. Other rules of the road include the prohibition of using a mobile phone, eating and dangling arms out of the window while driving. Driving shirtless and wearing backless shoes are also chargeable offences.

In Alicante and Murcia it is best to park in an underground car park. In other places, blue markings on the street mean you need to buy a ticket from a parking meter and display it in your windscreen.

The coastal motorway north of Alicante is toll paying but there is a free inland alternative via Alcoi (Alcoy). Most other *autovías* (dual carriageways) in the region are toll-free.

Speed limits, unless otherwise indicated, are 120 kmph (75 mph) on *autopistas* (toll motorways), 100 kmph (62 mph) on motorways with hardshoulders, 50 kmph (31 mph) in built-up areas and 90 kmph (56 mph) on all other roads.

Cycling

Leisure cycling is very popular in Spain and there are several green way routes in the region (see pp60–61). Minor roads, however, are not always well signposted and distances between towns can be long. Always wear a helmet and carry water with you. Bike hire is available in resorts and at rural hotels.

Walking

All the towns and villages in this region are best explored on foot. Alicante and Murcia are small enough to make public transport optional. The main sights in all the cities are clustered in the historic centres, and a stroll will throw up all kinds of delightful details that you might otherwise miss.

In the countryside, hikers are spoilt for choice; there are several National and Regional Parks with marked footpaths, as well as long-distance walking trails, such as the GR7 (see p61) and the GR92. When out walking, always tell somewhere where you are going, wear a hat and take plenty of water.

DIRECTORY

ARRIVING BY AIR

Alicante-Elche Airport
MAP E6
🖀 902 40 47 04
🌐 aena.es

easyJet
🌐 easyjet.com

Iberia
🖀 901 11 15 00
🌐 iberia.com

Jet2
🌐 jet2.com

Murcia-San Javier Airport
MAP P4
🖀 902 404 704
🌐 aena.es

Ryanair
🌐 ryanair.com

ARRIVING BY SEA

Algérie Ferries
🌐 algerieferries.dz

Balearia
🌐 balearia.com

INTERNATIONAL TRAIN TRAVEL

Renfe
🖀 902 32 03 20
🌐 renfe.com

SNCF
🌐 voyages-sncf.com
🌐 raileurope.com

LONG-DISTANCE BUS TRAVEL

Alicante Coach station
Muelle de Poniente
🌐 estacionalicante.es

Eurolines
🌐 eurolines.com

REGIONAL AND LOCAL TRAINS AND TRAMS

Alicante Tram
🖀 961 92 40 00
🌐 tramalicante.es

Renfe Feve
🌐 renfe.com/viajeros/feve

TAXIS

Radio Taxi Murcia
🖀 968 24 88 00
🌐 radiotaximurcia.com

Taxi Alicante
🖀 965 25 25 11
🌐 taxienalicante.com

Practical Information

Passports and Visas

For entry requirements, including visas, consult your nearest Spanish embassy or check the **Ministry for Foreign Affairs**. From late 2023, citizens of the UK, US, Canada, Australia and New Zealand do not need a visa for stays of up to three months, but must apply in advance for the European Travel Information and Authorization System (**ETIAS**). Visitors from other countries may also require an ETIAS, so check before travelling. EU nationals do not need a visa or an ETIAS.

Government Advice

Now more than ever, it is important to consult both your and the Spanish government's advice before travelling. The **UK Foreign, Commonwealth & Development Office (FCDO)**, the **US State Department**, the **Australian Department of Foreign Affairs and Trade** and the Ministry for Foreign Affairs offer the latest information on security, health and local regulations.

Customs Information

You can find information on the laws relating to goods and currency taken in or out of Spain on the **Turespaña** website.

Insurance

We recommend that you take out a comprehensive insurance policy covering theft, loss of belongings, medical care, cancellations and delays, and read the small print carefully.

UK citizens are eligible for free emergency medical care in Spain provided they have a valid European Health Insurance Card (EHIC) or UK Global Health Insurance Card (**GHIC**). For non-EU visitors, private insurance is highly recommended.

Dentistry may not be fully covered under a standard insurance policy, and can be expensive.

Health

Spain has a world-class healthcare system. In a medical emergency, dial the **Emergency Number** and ask for an ambulance. Good regional hospitals with accident and emergency facilities include **Hospital General Universitario de Alicante**, **Hospital General Universitario Morales Meseguer** and **Hospital Clínica Benidorm**.

Bring any prescription drugs you require with you in your hand baggage on the flight. Spanish medication may differ from your own in name, dosage and form, so you should bring the generic (rather than brand) name of your medicine with you in case you need a repeat prescription.

Spanish pharmacists are highly trained and can be very knowledgeable about minor ailments. Most major cities have at least one 24-hour *farmacia* (pharmacy). Its details are posted in all of the other pharmacy windows.

The Costa Blanca has a huge expat community, with multilingual doctors and dentists catering to all nationalities. Hotels and pharmacies can advise you. If you're using the EU reciprocal healthcare agreement, make sure the doctor belongs to the Spanish healthcare system: check before you accept treatment.

When travelling around Costa Blanca, visitors should beware of heatstroke, sunburn and dehydration. Always use sunscreen, wear a hat, and try to stay in the shade between noon and 4pm. Jellyfish stings are an occasional nuisance. Rinse them in fresh water with bicarbonate of soda.

For information regarding COVID-19 vaccination requirements, consult government advice.

Smoking, Alcohol and Drugs

Smoking is banned in enclosed public spaces and is a fineable offence, although you can still smoke on the terraces of bars and restaurants.

Public drinking is technically illegal in Spain. However, attitudes are generally relaxed and the law is rarely enforced; it is common to see people drinking on the street outside the bar of purchase.

Recreational drugs are illegal, and possession of even a very small quantity can lead to an extremely hefty fine. Amounts that suggest an intent to supply drugs to other people can lead to custodial sentences.

ID

By law you must carry identification with you at all times in Spain. A photocopy of your passport should usually suffice, but you may be asked to report to a police station with the original document.

Personal Security

Costa Blanca is a relatively safe place to visit, but petty crime does take place, particularly in high season. Pickpockets work known tourist areas, stations and beaches. Use your common sense and always be alert to your surroundings. It is wise to take necessary precautions such as locking your valuables in a hotel safety-deposit box and never taking them to the

beach. Don't leave anything visible in your car.

If you do have anything stolen, report the crime within 24 hours to the nearest police station and take your ID with you. Get a copy of the crime report *(denuncia)* in order to make an insurance claim. Contact your embassy if your passport is stolen, or in the event of a serious crime.

The Mediterranean flora dries up in summer and a carelessly discarded match or cigarette butt can set off a blaze that can soon rage out of control. Call the **Fire Brigade (Bomberos)** on the emergency number if you are concerned about a fire.

Spain has three police forces. The **Policía Nacional** deals with urban crime, so report anything stolen to them. The **Policía Local** deals with minor urban crime and traffic control. The

Guardia Civil polices the main highways and rural areas.

The **Servicio Marítimo de la Guardia Civil (SEMAR)** is responsible for search and rescue at sea.

As a rule, Spaniards are very accepting of all people, regardless or their race, gender or sexuality. Homosexuality was legalized in Spain in 1979 and in 2007, the government recognized same-sex marriage and the adoption rights of same-sex couples. LGBTQ+ friendly beaches, bars and other establishments can be found all around Costa Blanca. Benidorm is the region's main hub for LGBTQ+ travellers; its first LGBTQ+ bar opened in the 1960s and it now hosts an annual, week-long Pride Festival. If you do feel unsafe at any point, head for the nearest police station.

DIRECTORY

PASSPORTS AND VISAS

ETIAS
w etiasvisa.com

Ministry for Foreign Affairs
w exteriores.gob.es

GOVERNMENT ADVICE

Australian Department of Foreign Affairs and Trade
w dfat.gov.au
w smarttraveller.gov.au

UK Foreign, Commonwealth & Development Office (FCDO)
w gov.uk/foreign-travel-advice

US State Department
w travel.state.gov

CUSTOMS INFORMATION

Turespaña
w spain.info

INSURANCE

GHIC
w ghic.org.uk

HEALTH

Emergency Number
C 112

Hospital Clínica Benidorm
MAP G4 ■ Avda Alfonso Puchades, 03501 Benidorm C 965 85 38 50

Hospital General Universitario de Alicante
MAP E5 ■ Avda Pintor Baez 12, Alicante (Alacant) C 965 93 30 00

Hospital General Universitario Morales Meseguer
MAP N3 ■ Avda Marqués de los Vélez s/n, Murcia C 968 36 09 00

PERSONAL SECURITY

Fire Brigade (Bomberos)
C 080

Guardia Civil
C 062

Policía Local
C 092

Policía Nacional
C 091

Servicio Marítimo de la Guardia Civil (SEMAR)
C 900 20 22 02
w guardiacivil.es

Travellers with Specific Requirements

Tourism For All in the UK and **SATH** (Society f or Accessible Travel and Hospitality) in the US can provide information for those travelling with specific requirements.

Tourist offices on the Costa Blanca provide details of wheelchair-accessible hotels and sights. Restaurants do their best to support those with accessibility requirements, but it is wise to call in advance. There are some accessible beaches along the Costa Blanca that feature wheelchair ramps and floating chairs for hire; contact the local tourism office to find out more.

The Confederación Española de Personas con Discapacidad Física y Orgánica (**COCEMFE**) and **Accessible Spain Travel** provide information and tailored itineraries for those with reduced mobility, sight and hearing.

Spain's public transport system generally caters for all passengers, providing wheelchairs, adapted toilets, ramps and reserved car parking. Metro maps in Braille are available from the Organización Nacional de Ciegos (**ONCE**). Taxis specifically adapted for wheelchair users are available on request.

Time Zone

Eastern Spain is on Central European Time, which is an hour ahead of Greenwich Mean Time. Spain runs on daylight saving time from March to October.

Money

Spain is one of the many European countries using the euro (€), which is divided into 100 céntimos.

Money-changing facilities are available at the airports, and almost all banks offer exchange services. The outlets clustered in the resorts often charge a hefty commission. Banks in the area are usually open from 8:30am to 2pm Monday to Friday.

Cash machines (ATMs) can be found on almost every street corner in the city centres. Look for a sign saying "Telebanco". Instructions are posted onscreen in a variety of languages. Some Spanish banks charge a commission for using ATMs, and you will need to check whether your own bank will charge you.

You will find that major credit cards such as Visa and MasterCard are accepted in almost all shops, hotels, restaurants, tourist sights and train stations. American Express is generally less widely accepted. Some smaller towns and villages may not take card payments, however, so it is always advisable to have some cash on you.

Pre-paid currency cards are a useful alternative to debit and credit cards, and are a secure way of carrying money. They can be pre-loaded with euros, fixing exchange rates before you leave, and then used like a debit card at ATMs, bars, restaurants and shops. Contactless payments are common in Costa Blanca's main towns and resorts.

Spain does not have a big tipping culture, but it is appreciated and it's common to roundup the bill in restaurants.

Electrical Appliances

The electricity supply in Spain is AC 220 volts. Spanish plugs have two round pins. Travel adapters are widely available for the different types of plug but check that your appliance will work at this voltage.

Mobile Phones and Wi-Fi

Free Wi-Fi is reasonably common in Spain, particularly in libraries, large public spaces, restaurants and bars. Some places, such as airports and hotels, may charge for you to use their Wi-Fi.

Visitors travelling to Spain with EU tariffs are able to use their devices abroad without being affected by roaming charges. Users will be charged the same rates for data, calls and texts as at home.

Some UK networks have reintroduced roaming charges for their customers. Always check with your provider before you travel.

Postal Services

Correos is Spain's postal service. Postal rates fall into three price bands: Spain; Europe and North Africa; and the rest of the world. Parcels must be weighed and stamped at Correos offices, which are open from 8:30am to 9:30pm Monday to

Friday; outside the cities they close by 1–2pm on weekdays.

Letters sent from a post office usually arrive more quickly than if posted in a *buzón* (postbox). In cities, *buzóns* are yellow pillar boxes; in rural areas they are small, wall-mounted postboxes.

Weather

The peak holiday months are July and August, when temperatures peak and the weather is dry. During this time, you can expect to find large crowds of Spanish and international holiday-makers in the resorts and at popular sights.

Winter is mild and sunny during the day, with a few scattered showers throughout the season. This is a great to visit the Costa Blanca if you're interested in sightseeing.

Spring and early autumn find the countryside at its most lush. In these seasons it is possible (if a little cool) to swim in the sea, there's plenty of room on the beach and you will have a wider choice of accommodation.

Opening Hours

On public holidays, some bars and restaurants and most shops will be closed, especially in the more rural inland regions. The transport system runs restricted services. If the holiday falls midweek, it's common to take an extra day off, forming a long weekend known as a *puente* (bridge).

Many businesses, except those in the holiday resorts, are closed for the whole of August.

Most museums, public buildings and monuments are closed on Mondays.

Shops are usually open from 10am to 2pm and from 5pm to 8:30pm Monday to Saturday. Larger shops and department stores are open all day.

The COVID-19 pandemic proved that situations can change suddenly. Always check before visiting attractions and hospitality venues for up-to-date hours and booking requirements.

Visitor Information

Before your trip, you can contact the **UK Spanish National Tourist Office** or the **USA Spanish National Tourist Office** for helpful information on things to do and see around the Costa Blanca.

The slick and efficient Turespaña *(see p121)*, the body that promotes Spanish tourism, has a very good website that will give you general information about the area. Local tourism is organized by the regions and provinces of Spain (in this case **Alicante Tourist Office** and **Murcia Tourist Office**) and you'll find more useful information on their websites and at their regional tourist offices. Most towns now have their own good tourism websites with down-loadable brochures and maps. There are also many commercial web-sites covering the Costa Blanca but they cannot be relied on for comprehensive, impartial or up-to-date information.

DIRECTORY

TRAVELLERS WITH SPECIFIC REQUIREMENTS

Accessible Spain Travel
W accessiblespaintravel.com

COCEMFE
C 91 744 3600
W cocemfe.es

ONCE
W once.es

SATH
C 212 447 7284
W sath.org

Tourism For All
C 0845 124 9971
W tourismforall.org.uk

POSTAL SERVICES

Correos
C 915 197 197
W correos.es

VISITOR INFORMATION

Alicante Tourist Office
Rambla de Méndez Núñez 23
C 965 20 00 00
W costablanca.org

Murcia Tourist Office
Plaza Cardenal Belluga, Edificio Ayuntamiento
C 968 35 87 49
W murciaturistica.es

UK Spanish National Tourist Office
6th Floor, 64 North Row, London W1K 7DE
C 020 7317 2048

USA Spanish National Tourist Office
60 East 42nd Street, Suite 5300, New York, NY 1013
C 212 265 8822

Local Customs

A famous Spanish tradition is the siesta, a short nap usually taken after the midday meal and during the hottest part of the day. During the siesta period (between 2pm and 5pm), many shops close.

Bullfighting

Corridas (bullfights) are held on the Costa Blanca. Supporters argue that the bulls are bred for the industry and would be killed as calves were it not for bullfighting. Organizations such as the Asociación Defensa Derechos Animal (**ADDA**) hold protests against the bullfighting industry as they believe it leads to gratuitous cruelty towards animals.

If you do attend a *corrida*, bear in mind that it's better to see a big-name matador because they are more likely to make a clean and quick kill. The audience will make their disapproval evident if they don't.

Visiting Churches and Cathedrals

Spain retains a strong Catholic identity. Most churches and cathedrals will not permit visitors during Sunday Mass. Generally, entrance to churches is free, however a fee may apply to enter special areas, such as the cloisters.

When visiting religious buildings always ensure that you are dressed modestly, with knees and shoulders covered. Always turn your phone off or on silent and refrain from flash photography inside.

Languages

Alicante Province and the Costa Blanca are part of the Autonomous Community of Valencia, where the two official languages are Valencian (related to Catalan) and Spanish (Castilian). While some people may prefer to speak Valencian (except in Alicante, where Spanish is always more prominent), most also speak Spanish and signs are always bilingual. In the province of Murcia, only Spanish is spoken. English is widely spoken in cities and tourist resorts, but not always in rural areas. Locals will appreciate you attempting a few niceties in Valencian or Spanish.

Taxes and Refunds

Value-added tax (IVA in Spanish) in mainland Spain is normally 21 per cent, but with lower rates for certain goods and services. Non-EU citizens are entitled to claim back IVA on goods and services costing over €90. You will need to show your passport in the shop and get a stamped receipt that shows the IVA component. If you present this at your departure airport you'll then get a refund of the tax paid.

Shopping

A useful one-stop place to shop is the big department store **El Corte Inglés**, which has branches, including a supermarket, in Alicante and Murcia.

Almost every town has a weekly market selling an array of local produce along with all kinds of cheap clothes, kitchen implements and, sometimes, handicrafts and souvenirs. Many of the larger towns and resorts have covered markets open daily (except Sundays), selling fresh produce. There are also regular craft markets on summer evenings along much of the coast.

The annual sales (look for signs saying *rebaixes* or *rebajas*) are held in January and July or August. Most of the major stores have a section devoted to *oportunidades*, where you can pick up bargains if you're prepared to rummage. Haggling is not acceptable in shops, but you can bargain for crafts at market stalls.

Dining

The word restaurant can cover many things in Spain, from informal beach bars to extremely formal, costly and perhaps even Michelin-starred places, where you'll be expected to dress quite smartly for dinner.

The main meal of the day is lunch, which typically begins at 2pm and can last a couple of hours. It tends to consist of three courses with a glass or two of wine. The Spanish like to take their time over lunch and many people have a siesta afterwards.

Breakfast, in contrast, is a light and hurried affair – perhaps a pastry or a croissant washed down with *café con leche* (milky coffee). Most hotels on the coast offer a buffet-style breakfast that accommodates visitors of all nationalities. Dinner is also "late". The Spanish don't eat properly until around 9pm. They may fill the gap between lunch and dinner with *merienda* (an afternoon snack), which is usually something sweet. Many restaurants, including those in the resorts, are closed on Sunday or Monday nights.

At all times of day, hunger can be kept at bay with a round of tapas in a local bar *(see pp68–9)*. The *tapeo*, a kind of bar crawl from tapas bar to tapas bar, is an institution in Alicante (Alacant) and Murcia City. If you want a larger portion, ask for a *ración*. Often you will be asked to point to what you want at the bar, and everything is added up when you are ready to leave.

On weekday lunchtimes many restaurants offer a fixed-price *menú del día*, geared towards local working people. It usually includes two or three courses with bread and a glass of wine, and is very good value, even at some of the smarter restaurants.

Vegetarians can have a tricky time in Spain, where even apparently innocuous vegetable dishes are regularly flavoured with ham or chorizo. There are a few vegetarian restaurants, but these are mainly only in the cities. Every bar or restaurant will make an effort to feed you if you say exactly what you want.

Accommodation

Spain offers a range of accommodation. A useful list of accommodation can be found on the Turespaña *(see p121)* website. Hotel rates vary depending on the season. Visitors should aim to book accommodation well in advance if they plan to visit in the peak, and most expensive, season (July and August) or during a public holiday.

Package holidays are big business on the Costa Blanca, with some incredibly low-priced deals.

Paradores (paradors) are state-run hotels. They tend to be fairly pricey, but have good facilities. While in other parts of Spain they often occupy historic buildings, the two on the Costa Blanca are both purpose-built: Xàbia *(see p126)* on the Costa Blanca and next to the castle in Lorca in inland Murcia *(see p126)*. Look out for special deals on the **Paradors** website.

Casas rurales – country houses for rent (or sometimes offering B&B) – are growing in popularity in Spain. Often located in small inland villages, they vary hugely in terms of accommodation and facilities but the price is invariably cheaper than a self-catering coastal villa.

Numerous companies offer self-catering villa rentals, ranging from simple apartments to quasi-palaces. Websites such as **Toprural** and **Vrbo** are the best places to look.

Some smaller hotels are known as *hostales*. This is not the same thing as hostel in English; it simply denotes a cheaper place to stay with fewer facilities than the average hotel. *Pensiones* are similar to *hostales*, offering basic amenities at affordable prices.

Backpackers can find youth hostels (sometimes known as *albergues*) on websites such as **Hostelworld**. There are three youth hostels in Alicante, two in Murcia and one in Xàbia (Jávea).

A good-value option is camping and caravanning, and both are popular on the Costa Blanca. Sites are graded by a star system (one to three) according to the facilities offered. Many of the larger sites have great facilities, while inland sites are often less grand. Although prices vary according to facilities and proximity to the beach, they are generally cheap. However, if you have a car, a tent and more than two people, the site fees can add up to nearly as much as an inexpensive hotel room.

Most hotels quote their prices without including tax (IVA), which is 10 per cent in mainland Spain.

Places to Stay

PRICE CATEGORIES

For a standard, double room per night (with breakfast if included), taxes and extra charges.

....

€ under €100   €€ €100–200   €€€ over €200

Luxury Hotels

Hostería de Mont Sant, Xàtiva (Játiva)

MAP E1 ▪ Subida al Castillo s/n ▪ 962 27 50 81 ▪ www.mont-sant. com ▪ €€

A former monastery tucked below Xàtiva's castle is the idyllic setting for this romantic hotel which features a pool, gym, sauna and an elegant restaurant serving regional dishes (see p87).

Hotel Amérigo, Alicante (Alacant)

MAP U3 ▪ C/Rafael Altamira 7 ▪ 965 14 65 70 ▪ www.hospes.com ▪ €€€

Somewhat incongruously, the Amérigo is located in a tastefully renovated former Dominican convent. Its rooftop terrace features a heated plunge pool and enjoys impressive views of the Castillo de Santa Bárbara and the Old Town.

Hotel La Manga Príncipe Felipe, nr Cartagena

MAP P5 ▪ Los Belones ▪ 968 33 12 34 ▪ www. lamangaclub.com ▪ €€

In the heart of a premier golf resort, this hotel is a favourite with sports stars and celebrities. It is also well suited to families and has a Junior Club offering babysitting and activities for children aged 3 months to 12 years.

Hotel El Montiboli, La Vila Joiosa (Villajoyosa)

MAP F4 ▪ Partida Montiboli s/n ▪ 965 89 02 50 ▪ www.montiboli. com ▪ €€€

Perched on a rocky bluff overlooking a pretty cove, the Montiboli has airy rooms with terraces, as well as suites and bungalows. There is a wellness area with three pools. The restaurant with sea views offers superb Mediterranean cuisine.

Hotel Village Spa El Rodat, Xàbia (Jávea)

MAP H3 ▪ C/Murciana 9 ▪ 966 47 07 10 ▪ https:// elrodathotelvillagespa. com-hotel.com ▪ €€

This hotel, close to several golf courses, offers cosy rooms, suites and villas set in jasmine-scented gardens. There is a spa and pools (one indoor and one outside) overlooking the peak of Montgó.

Parador de Lorca

MAP K4 ▪ Castillo de Lorca ▪ 968 40 60 47 ▪ www.parador.es ▪ €€

Adjacent to the castle and built over an archaeological site, this modern, well-equipped hotel is a little way from the town centre and somewhat lacking in atmosphere but this is made up for by the indoor pool and spa facilities, spacious rooms and grounds, and the quality of its restaurant.

Asia Gardens Hotel and Thai Spa, Benidorm

MAP G4 ▪ Avda Alcalde Eduardo Zaplana Hernández-Soro ▪ 966 81 84 00 ▪ www.asiagardens. es ▪ €€€

Set amid tropical gardens dotted with pretty waterfalls and pools, this is an enormous luxury hotel. Facilities include several restaurants and a relaxing Thai spa.

Parador de Xàbia (Jávea)

MAP H3 ▪ Avda del Mediterráneo 233 ▪ 965 79 02 00 ▪ www.parador. es ▪ €€€

This 1970s four-star *parador* has a stunning setting right on the beach, and is surrounded by lush gardens. The large, light rooms have terraces with sea views. Facilities include pool, gym and sauna. There's a fine restaurant.

SH Villa Gadea Hotel, Altea

MAP G4 ▪ Partida de Villa Gadea ▪ 966 81 71 00 ▪ www.sh-hoteles. com ▪ €€€

In the hilltop village of Altea (see p48), this hotel with fine sea views offers three lagoon-style pools, tennis courts, a children's club and thalasso-spa. Dine in any one of five different restaurants.

Villa Venecia Hotel Boutique, Benidorm

MAP G4 ▪ Plaza San Juan 1 ▪ 965 88 54 66 ▪ www. hotelvillavenecia.com ▪ €€€

Amazing sea views mark this gorgeous five-star

hideaway on a hilltop that is just a short walk from Benidorm's charming old town. The staff are friendly and facilities include a restaurant, a spa and a pool.

Costa Blanca Hotels

Gran Hotel Sol y Mar, Calp (Calpe)

MAP G4 ▪ Calle de Benidorm 3 ▪ 965 87 50 55 ▪ www.granhotel solymar.com ▪ €€

This huge seafront resort hotel, for guests aged 16 and over, provides a choice of accommodation ranging from rooms to self-catering apartments. Also available are a spa, swimming pools and a restaurant.

Hostal Loreto, Dénia (Denia)

MAP H2 ▪ C/Loreto 12 ▪ 966 43 54 19 ▪ www. hostalloreto.com ▪ €

A congenial, family-run hotel tucked away in Dénia's pretty old quarter, it is housed in a former convent dating back more than four centuries. The rooms are modest but well equipped, and some have balconies.

Hotel Jávea, Xàbia

MAP H3 ▪ C/Pío X 5 ▪ 965 79 54 61 ▪ www.hotel-javea.com ▪ €€

Just steps from the old port, this classic seaside hotel has friendly staff and spotless rooms, some with balconies overlooking the port and pebbly beach.

Hotel Bonalba, Mutxamel

MAP E5 ▪ C/Vespre 10 ▪ 965 95 95 95 ▪ www. hotelbonalba.com ▪ €€

The Hotel Bonalba makes an excellent base from

which to discover the Costa Blanca. Facilities on offer here include a spa and sauna, outdoor and indoor pools, and beauty treatments. The hotel is surrounded by a fine 18-hole golf course.

Hotel Boutique, Isla Tabarca

MAP E6 ▪ C/Arzola s/n ▪ 966 29 28 00 ▪ www. boutiqueislatabarca.com-hotel.com ▪ €

The austere 18th-century governor's house on this little island just off the coast from Santa Pola has been converted into a charming small hotel, with 15 simple, airy rooms. It has a café-bar for drinks and light meals. The hotel can arrange various kinds of watersports.

Hotel Cibeles Playa, Gandía-Playa

MAP F1 ▪ C/Clot de la Mota 9 ▪ 962 84 80 83 ▪ www.hotelcibeles.com ▪ €€

Just a 2-minute walk from the beach, this glassy, modern complex offers air-conditioned rooms with stunning coastal views from the balconies. It also has a buffet restaurant and a swimming pool.

Hotel Levante Club & Spa, Benidorm

MAP G3 ▪ Avda Severa Ochoa 3B ▪ 965 86 09 56 ▪ www.hotellevanteclub. com ▪ €€

With a large spa, an outdoor pool and bright, spacious rooms, this friendly, ultra-modern hotel for over-16s is located a very short walk away from the beautiful Levante Beach.

Hotel La Serena, Altea

MAP G4 ▪ C/Alba 10 ▪ 966 88 58 49 ▪ www. hoteleslaserena.com ▪ €€

This exquisite, small, adults-only hotel offers simple, stylish rooms, an outdoor pool and a hammam (Turkish bath). The organic breakfast here must not be missed.

Hotel Swiss Moraira, Moraira-Teulada

MAP G3 ▪ C/Haya 175 ▪ 965 74 71 04 ▪ www. swisshotelmoraira.com ▪ €€

Relax amid the extensive gardens, take a dip in the swimming pool or treat yourself to spa session at this luxurious hotel. A range of packages, including yoga and a gourmet dining experience can be arranged by the very helpful team of staff.

Kaktus Albir, Albir

MAP G4 ▪ Paseo De Las Estrellas 11 ▪ 966 86 48 30 ▪ www.kaktusgrup. com ▪ €€

This pleasant complex right in front of the beach has an expansive pool and lovely gardens. The hotel also has a fitness centre with an indoor pool and hot tub as well as a buffet-style restaurant.

Posada del Mar, Dénia

MAP H2 ▪ Plaza Drassanes 2 ▪ 966 43 29 66 ▪ www. laposadadelmar.com ▪ €€

A medieval mansion has been restored to house this stylish hotel, with 16 rooms and nine suites, some with spectacular terraces. Each room is individually decorated with an elegant mixture of old and new.

La Sella Golf Resort and Spa, Dénia (Denia)

MAP H2 ▪ Partida Alquería Ferrando s/n ▪ 966 45 40 54 ▪ www. lasellagolfresort.com ▪ €€

With a view over the prestigious La Sella golf course in the foothills of the Montgó Natural Park, this is one of the most luxurious resorts in the whole region. The spa is one of the finest in Spain.

Oliva Nova Beach & Golf Resort, Oliva

MAP G2 ▪ Avda Dalí 4 ▪ 962 85 79 44 ▪ www. olivanova.com ▪ €€€

A handsome seafront complex, the Oliva Nova is set around an impressive, Ballesteros-designed, 18-hole golf course. Most rooms and suites have sea views. Some even have private pools.

Costa Cálida Hotels

Hospederia Los Balcones, Mazarrón

MAP M5 ▪ Paraje los Balcones, 187, Cañadas del Romero, Mazarrón ▪ 639 32 38 08 ▪ www. hospederiaruralthe balcones.com ▪ €

There is a swimming pool, a restaurant and free Wi-Fi access at this small hotel in a restored old country house. The complex includes trekking and off-road cycling routes. It also serves as a training centre for motorcross.

Hotel Al Sur, Calabardina

MAP L6 ▪ C/Torre de Cope 24 ▪ 608 17 89 76 ▪ €

Located in a quiet village, this is a a delightful hotel. Arches and terraces give it a seductive Arabic feel. There is no restaurant nor pool, but quiet beaches are just steps away, and there are plenty of local places to eat and drink.

Hotel Mayarí, Calabardina

MAP L6 ▪ Río de Janeiro 14 ▪ 968 41 97 48 ▪ www. hotel-mayari.com ▪ €

Perched on a hill below Cabo Cope, this hotel offers commanding views from its attractive rooms and lovely terraces. Explore the surroundings with the free bikes that the hotel provides.

Atrium, Mazarrón

MAP M5 ▪ Avenida Antonio Segado del Olmo 20 Bolnuevo, Mazarrón ▪ www.atriumhotel.es ▪ 968 15 83 83 ▪ €€

Most of the rooms have sea views at this small hotel. There is a restaurant, and two family suites have kitchenettes. Outside is a Jacuzzi, which you can use at night as well as during the day.

Balneario La Encarnación, Los Alcázares

MAP P4 ▪ C/Condesa 8 ▪ 968 57 50 07 ▪ www. balneariolaencarnacion. es ▪ €€

Entering this former spa hotel on the Mar Menor is like stepping back in time. The chic rooms have old-world charm, and the service is courteous and old-fashioned.

Gaviotas, Murcia

MAP Q4 ▪ Gran Via La Manga de Mar Menor ▪ 968 337 289 ▪ www. hotelania.com ▪ €€

This functional modern beach resort hotel with sea views is situated between the Mar Menor and the Mediterranean. All rooms have Wi-Fi. There are several bars, restaurants, shops and other facilities close by.

Lodomar, San Pedro del Pinatar

MAP P3 ▪ Río Bidasoa 1 ▪ 968 18 68 02 ▪ www. hotellodomar.com ▪ €€

The Lodomar is a vast complex of rooms and apartments, with a gym, pools and a spa special-izing in thalassotherapy. The hotel sits on the edge of the San Pedro del Pinatar Regional Park, a paradise for bird-watchers. The Mar Menor beaches are about 500 m (547 yards) away.

Puerto Juan Montiel, Águilas

MAP L6 ▪ Avenida del Puerto Deportivo 1, Playa de Poniente, Águilas ▪ 968 493 493 ▪ www.hotelpuerto juanmontiel.com ▪ €€€

Lovers of watersports will enjoy this seafront hotel. It stands next to a 355-berth marina in which there is a diving school.

City Hotels

The Cathedral Hostel, Murcia

MAP U5 ▪ Calle Trapería 19 (3rd floor), Murcia ▪ 968 93 00 07 ▪ www.the cathedralhostel.com ▪ €

The only youth hostel set in an old building in the centre of Murcia stands near the cathedral, as its name suggests. It has a common room, a shared kitchen, air-conditioning, free Wi-Fi, bike storage and wheelchair access.

Los Habaneros, Cartagena

MAP P5 ▪ C/ San Diego 60 ▪ 968 50 52 50 ▪ www.hotelhabaneros cartagena.com ▪ €

Sitting at the entrance to old Cartagena, this classic hotel is excellent value. The rooms are comfortable and the restaurant is well regarded.

Hostel Olé, Alicante (Alacant)

MAP T2 ▪ Calle Poeta Quintana 26 ▪ 966 14 52 06 ▪ www.hostelole. com ▪ €

This city-centre youth hostel is still only a 10-minute walk from the beach. Reasonably priced food is served in the dining room. Bikes and Segways can be rented at the hostel, and there is a 24-hour reception.

Zenit Murcia

MAP T6 ▪ Plaza San Pedro 5–6 ▪ 968 21 47 42 ▪ www.zenit hoteles.com ▪ €

Situated next to the Plaza de las Flores, this is one of the city's best bargains. Rooms are well equipped, and the bathrooms are stuffed with goodies. There's a great bar and a restaurant offering Mediterranean dishes, and staff are unfailingly helpful and courteous.

Hotel Les Monges Palace, Alicante

MAP U2 ▪ C/San Agustín 4 ▪ 965 21 50 46 ▪ www. hotellesmonges.es ▪ €€

Book early for this cute and wonderfully quirky *pensión*, housed in a former convent in the heart of the old city. The corridors are lined with works of art (including

a Dalí sketch), and some rooms have Jacuzzis or four-posters.

NH Cartagena

MAP P5 ▪ Plaza Héroes de Cavite 2 ▪ 968 12 09 08 ▪ www.nh-hoteles.es ▪ €€

Part of a reliable chain, this hotel is located in Cartagena's midtown. Rooms are stylish and modern, with Wi-Fi and air-conditioning. The restaurant, NHube, serves traditional Spanish fare.

Sercotel Spa Porta Maris & Suites del Mar, Alicante

MAP E5 ▪ Plaza Puerta del Mar 3 ▪ 965 14 70 21 ▪ www.sercotelhoteles. com ▪ €€€

A great city-centre option, this hotel on the seafront by Alicante's port has spacious bedrooms (including family rooms) with large terraces offering views over the bay. The resort has an enormous pool, a wellness centre and a restaurant.

Tryp by Wyndham Rincón de Pepe, Murcia

MAP U6 ▪ C/Apóstoles 34 ▪ 968 21 22 39 ▪ www. melia.com ▪ €€

Set in a historic building, the renovated rooms here are minimalist and spacious. The hotel has an excellent restaurant and tapas bar (see p71).

Rural Retreats

Finca El Tossal, Bollula

MAP G3 ▪ Partida La Foya 5 ▪ 965 97 21 83 ▪ www. finca-el-tossal.com ▪ €

Set in the hills behind Altea, this rosy *finca* (farmhouse) has been

sympathetically restored. Stylish rooms, luxuriant gardens, a large pool and heavenly views make this a great choice.

Hospedería Rural Molino de Felipe, Mula

MAP L2 ▪ Paraje Ribera de los Molinos ▪ 968 66 20 13 ▪ www.hotelrural mula.com ▪ €

One of the last working flour mills in Spain (dating back to the 16th century), this is also a wonderful hotel. There's excellent walking to be had in the nearby Parque Regional de Sierra Espuña. The hotel also has a gym and pool.

Hotel La Façana, Biar

MAP D4 ▪ Plaza de la Constitución 2 ▪ 965 81 03 73 ▪ www.lafasana. com ▪ €

This rural hotel offers nine charming rooms (two of them are triples) right in the centre of Biar; all of them have views of the church and the town hall. The excellent on-site restaurant serves a range of local delicacies.

Mas Fontanelles, Biar

MAP D4 ▪ Ctra Biar-Bañeres Km 4, Biar ▪ 686 42 61 26 ▪ www. masfontanelles.com ▪ €

A beautiful rural hotel situated 4 km (2 miles) from the little village of Biar, it has eight simple, individually decorated rooms, extensive gardens and an outdoor pool. It's also a great base for hiking and other outdoor activities. Dinners (including vegetarian meals) can be served on request.

For a key to hotel price categories see p126

El Molino del Río Argos, nr Caravaca de la Cruz

MAP K2 ▪ Camino Viejo de Archivel ▪ 968 43 33 81 ▪ www.molinodelrio.com ▪ €

A 16th-century mill on the banks of the River Argos has been converted to house six apartments and one double room. There is a pool, a terrace with cooling fountains, several lush orchards, and endless rolling sierras.

Pensión Castells, Castell de Castells

MAP F3 ▪ C/San Vicente 18 ▪ 965 51 82 54 ▪ www.mountainholidays-spain.com ▪ €

This utterly charming mountain inn is run by a friendly British couple. Delicious local cuisine is accompanied by wine straight from the barrel. Also on offer are tailor-made walking, biking and activity holidays.

Casa del Maco, Benissa

MAP G3 ▪ Pou Roig 15 ▪ 965 73 28 42 ▪ www.casadelmaco.com ▪ €€

Located in the foothills of the Lleus Valley, this luxurious country hideaway has just four rooms, each with beamed ceilings. There's a large terrace and a refreshing pool. Casa del Maco's romantic restaurant serves fine French cuisine with Mediterranean and Belgian influences.

El Cortijo Villa Rosa, Caravaca de la Cruz

MAP K2 ▪ Paraje Chuecos ▪ 968 70 87 63 ▪ www.cortijovillarosa.com ▪ €€

Just outside the village of Caravaca de la Cruz is this complex of four farmhouses. Each has been lovingly restored to offer rustic charm with modern comfort. There are pools, a BBQ area and lovely grounds.

Hotel Casa Lehmi, Tàrbena

MAP G3 ▪ Partida El Buscarró 1–3 ▪ 965 88 40 18 ▪ www.casa lehmi.com ▪ €€

A beautifully restored little finca set amid mountains about 30 km (19 miles) from the coast. There are eight spacious and elegant rooms in an adjoining annexe. The excellent facilities here include a welcoming pool, a tennis court and a sauna.

Hotel Cases Noves, Guadalest

MAP F3 ▪ Calle de la Achova 2 ▪ 965 88 53 09 ▪ www.hotelrural enalicante.es ▪ €€

This charming adults-only hotel is a great place to stay with its four tastefully decorated rooms, a spa and the terrace providing some wonderful views over the surrounding hills. Delicious, home-cooked food is served in the restaurant.

Hotel Castell de la Solana, Alcalalí

MAP G3 ▪ Crta a Pedreguer – Alcalalí, km 42, Pda La Coma ▪ 966 48 27 05 ▪ www.castelldela solana.es ▪ €€

Set amid lush olive groves at the foot of a mountain, this country hotel has just seven individually decorated rooms, two of which are wheelchair-accessible. There's a small spa, peaceful gardens and an outdoor pool. Over-14s only.

Hotel L'Estació, Bocairent

MAP D3 ▪ Parc de l'Estació ▪ 962 35 00 00 ▪ www.hotelestacio.com ▪ €€

This hotel is set in a former railway, near the Sierra de Mariola. One room is adapted for guests with physical disabilities. Aromatherapy kits and fruit baskets are included in each room.

Casa Rural Bons Aires, Alicante

MAP E3 ▪ Partida Llacunes, 6 ▪ 660 66 67 68 ▪ www.casabon saires.com ▪ €

Set in the Parque Natural de Font Roja, this adults-only retreat provides all that's needed for a tranquil holiday. Unwind in the outdoor pool, solarium, lovely gardens or in the cosy living area. Breakfast is included.

Hotel Termas, Archena

MAP M2 ▪ Balneario de Archena ▪ 968 68 80 22 ▪ www.balneario dearchena.com ▪ €€

The oldest and grandest hotel in this palm-shaded spa village offers comfortable rooms, but its public areas are redolent of a glorious past. It also offers health and beauty packages that include massages, reflexology and thalassotherapy.

Masía la Mota, Alcoi (Alcoy)

MAP E3 ▪ Ctra de la Font Roja 5 ▪ 966 54 03 70 ▪ www.masia lamota.com ▪ €€

This 18th-century farmhouse has been converted into an enchanting rural hotel and offers breathtaking views of the Sierra Carrascal de la Font Roja.

Vivood Landscape Hotel, Benimantell

MAP F3 ■ Carretara Guadalest-Alcoi 10 ■ 96 631 85 85 ■ www.vivood. com ■ €€€

An adults-only eco-hotel in the hills near Guadalest with a lounge bar and restaurant. Vegetarians and vegans are catered for with advance notice. Treats include Reiki sessions and massages.

Camping and Caravanning

Çamping Bella Vista, Águilas

MAP L6 ■ Ctra de la Vera Km 3 ■ 968 44 91 51 ■ www.campingbella vista.com ■ €

A big, friendly site 300 m (984 ft) from the beach, with a shop, a children's play area, table tennis, and a bar-restaurant close by. Wheelchair-accessible bungalows are available.

Camping Los Delfines, Playa Mojón

MAP M5 ■ Ctra Isla Plana, Playa Mojón, Puerto de Mazarrón ■ 968 59 45 27 ■ www.campinglos delfines.com ■ €

This large site has big pitches on the beach near Puerto de Mazarrón resort. It also rents out bungalows, includes entry to the thermal spa in summer and is fully accessible.

Camping El Jardín, El Campello

MAP E5 ■ C/Severo Ochoa 39 ■ 965 65 75 80 ■ www. campingeljardin.com ■ €

Close to glorious San Juan beach, this site has all the

usual amenities. There are few trees for shade, so get to the beach early in summer.

Camping La Marina, La Marina

MAP Q2 ■ Ctra N-332 Km 76 ■ 965 41 92 00 ■ www. lamarinaresort.com ■ €

This huge campsite in a seaside resort south of Santa Pola has every facility, ranging from children's play areas, a gym and a large pool with cascades, jacuzzi, and a water park, to a hairdresser and medical staff.

Camping Mariola, nr Bocairent

MAP D3 ■ Ctra Bocairent-Alcoi Km 9 ■ 962 13 51 60 ■ www.campingmariola. com ■ €

Set amid mountains and almond groves, this pretty site has shady pitches and cabins for rent. Activities on offer in the area include hiking, quad rental, and hot-air ballooning.

Camping Villasol, Benidorm

MAP G4 ■ Avda Bernat de Sarriá 13 ■ 965 85 04 22 ■ www.camping-villasol. com ■ €

Close to the beach, this large campsite is a virtual village. Facilities include two pools (one heated in winter), bars, a restaurant, supermarket, laundry and play areas. The site also rents out mobile homes.

Camping Xàtiva (Játiva)

MAP E1 ■ Ctra Genovés–Xàtiva ■ 658 42 83 02 ■ €

This pretty site, just outside historic Xàtiva, has a fabulous pool, lots of shady pitches and a laundry. It's a great base for

mountain biking, hiking or sightseeing.

Caravaning La Manga

MAP P5 ■ La Manga: Ctra Cartagena–La Manga, exit 11 ■ 968 56 30 14 ■ www.caravaning.es ■ €

This large campsite goes up to the shore of the Mar Menor. Along with camping and caravanning pitches, there are wooden bungalows for rent. Amenities include an indoor pool, laundry, supermarket, sauna and gym. There is also an outdoor cinema in summer.

La Puerta, Moratalla

MAP K1 ■ Ctra La Puerta ■ 968 73 00 08 ■ www. campinglapuerta.com ■ €

Set among trees close to the river, this campsite in a sleepy medieval village has tent and caravan pitches as well as cabins. Facilities include a bar, restaurant, supermarket and laundry.

Sierra Espuña

MAP L3 ■ Visitor Centre (Centro Ricardo Cordorníu): Parque Regional de Sierra Espuña; 968 43 14 30; www.sierraespuna.com ■ Camping Sierra Espuña: El Berro; 968 66 80 38; www.campingsierra espuna.com; €

There are three very basic camping areas within the stunning Parque Regional de Sierra Espuña; apart from four mountain refuges (see p27), they are the only options in the park itself, and must be booked in advance from the Visitor Centre. Just outside the park, Camping Sierra Espuña has many facilities, including wooden cabañas for rent.

For a key to hotel price categories see p126

Index

Acknowledgments

This edition updated by

Contributor Lynnette McCurdy

Senior Editor Alison McGill

Senior Art Editor Vinita Venugopal

Project Editors Dipika Dasgupta, Lucy Sara-Kelly

Art Editor Bandana Paul

Assistant Editor Ilina Choudhary

Picture Research Administrator Vagisha Pushp

Picture Research Manager Taiyaba Khatoon

Publishing Assistant Halima Mohammed

Jacket Designer Jordan Lambley

Cartographer Ashif Ashif

Senior Cartographer Subhashree Bharati

Cartography Manager Suresh Kumar

DTP Designer Rohit Rojal

Senior DTP Designer Tanveer Zaidi

Senior Production Editor Jason Little

Senior Production Controller Samantha Cross

Deputy Managing Editor Beverly Smart

Managing Editors Shikha Kulkarni, Hollie Teague

Managing Art Editor Sarah Snelling

Senior Managing Art Editor Priyanka Thakur

Art Director Maxine Pedliham

Publishing Director Georgina Dee

DK would like to thank the following for their contribution to the previous editions: Mary-Ann Gallagher, Nick Inman, Clare Peel, Helen Peters

The publisher would like to thank the following for their kind permission to reproduce their photographs:

Key: a-above; b-below/bottom; c-centre; f-far; l-left; r-right; t-top

123RF.com: Antonio Balaguer Soler 6cla.

4Corners: Richard Taylor 54cl.

Alamy Stock Photo: 1Apix 35crb; age fotostock 20cl, 27tr, 53tr, / Salva Garrigues 65bl; Alfie1981 102cl, 103cl; Arco Images GmbH 29tl; Dave Baxter 84b; Ignacio Perez Bayona 110c; Craig Joiner Photography 59cl; Stuart Crump 107cb, 113b; Guy Dry 75tr; Josie Elias 17bl, 94tl;

Factofoto 63tl; Mick Flynn 65tr; Nick Gregory 27bl; Peter Horree 110tl; imageBROKER 4cl, 32clb, 33tl, 58b, 73tr, 78tl, 78clb, 86clb; JTB Media Creation Inc. 91bl; Kim Kaminski 59tr; kolvenbach 52bl; Lanmas 80cl; Alfredo Maiquez 88tl; Tim Moore 61tr; Nature Picture Library 53cl; Natureworld 47bl; Richard Naude 31tl; Alberto Paredes 41c; Dave Porter 62cla; Prisma by Dukas Presseagentur GmbH, 83b; Dirk Renckhoff 74cla; REUTERS 62b; Martin Richardson 60clb; Russell Mills Travel 90clb; SCFotos - Stuart Crump Visuals 105crb; simo 105tl; Slick Shoots 92cla; Diane Stoney 86tr; Kevin Wheal 73br; Julie Woodhouse 42b.

AWL Images: Ivan Vdovin 4cla.

Costa Blanca Tourism Board: 11crb, 40t, 41tr, 75cl, 90tr.

Depositphotos Inc: diamant24 66ca.

Dreamstime.com: Steve Allen 23bl; Andreirybachuk 72t; Leonid Andronov 14-5, 28-9; Annegordon 30-1; Belahoche 95cl; Canettistock 43tr; Chasdesign1983 82cb; Clickandphoto 66br; Gerónimo Contreras Flores 54b; Craigolet 21bc; Diamant24 66cl; Diggerman 55tr; Serban Enache 69bl; Elena Fedulova 6crb, 31crb; Denis Fefilov 50tr; Iakov Filimonov 19cr, 24-5, 34-5, 57cl; Fotomicar 44b; Veronika Galkina 18br; Gbfoto 45cla; Hans Geel 115bl; Kalman89 10cl; Denis Kelly 89tr; Vadim Khomyakov 7tr; Pavel Kirichenko 16cb; Sergii Koval 85cr; La Fabrika Pixel S.l. 49cl; Daniël Leppens 30br; Luisangel70 15cr, 19bc, 82tl; Lunamarina 4t, 4crb, 10cra, 12-3, 48t, 48bl, 61b, 69cr, 73clb, 80b, 98-9, 101br, 104b, 106t; Dariya Maksimova 110-1; Larisa Matrosova 68bl; Antonio Ballesteros Mijailov 15tl; Mikelane45 26bc; Milacroft 52t; Mirko Moscatelli 7br; Alexander Mychko 67br; Olegmit 57br; Pathastings 69tr; Paulgrecaud 11c; Olaf Speier 10clb, 51tr; Sportphoto1 14cra; Tagore75 67tl; Tuulijumala 20-1; Typhoonski 96b; Vdvtut 2tr, 36-7, 74b; Tatyana Vychegzhanina 68t; Sergii Zinko 16t.

El Misteri d'Anna: 70b.

Getty Images: Bloomberg 64t; Chris Hepburn 109l; Ipsumpix 38b; JoWeb

Images 56t; Gerard Julien 39br; Quim Llenas 13cra; Calle Montes 45br; pabloarias imágenes 17tr; José Fuste Raga 4b; Moment / Allard Schager 1; A Richard Poolton Image 93b; Eloy Rodriguez 44cla; Universal History Archive 38tl, 39cl; UniversalImages Group 20br; www.luisguijarro.com 58tr.

iStockphoto.com: Leonid Andronov 3tr, 116-17; balalaich 35bl; danieldefotograaf 10b; FevreDream 2tl, 8-9; holgs 11br; OlafSpeier 3tl, 76-7; pabkov 50-1; SteveAllenPhoto 29cr.

Palau Ducal: 11clb, 32br, 32-3.

Quique Dacosta: 71cb.

Real Casino: 46bl.

Robert Harding Picture Library: Barbara Boensch 81cl; Alfredo Maiquez 43cl; Jose Fuste Raga 108cla; Antonio Real 26-7; Michael Snell 112cla.

SuperStock: age fotostock 11cra, 97c, / Yoko Aziz 4clb, / Tolo Balaguer 41bl, / Luis Domingo 13tl, 102b, / Craig Joiner 49tr, / Dragomir Nikolov 100ca, / Antonio Real 12br, / SCFotos / Stuart Crump 101tr, 114clb, / Jan Wlodarczyk 55cl; imageBROKER 18-9, 22-3, 23cra, 47t; Prisma / Raga Jose Fuste 4cr; J avier Marina 79cra; Robertharding 42ca; Travel Library Limited 56bl.

Cover

Front and spine: **Getty Images:** Moment / Allard Schager

Back: **Getty Images:** Moment / Allard Schager b, / Photo by Alex Tihonov tl; **iStockphoto.com:** Natalia Arteeva tr; E+ / fcafotodigital cla, Vladislav Zolotov crb

Pull Out Map Cover
Getty Images: Moment / Allard Schager

All other images © Dorling Kindersley

For further information see: www. dkimages.com

Commissioned Photography Tony Souter

Penguin Random House

First edition 2005

Published in Great Britain by Dorling Kindersley Limited DK, One Embassy Gardens, 8 Viaduct Gardens, London SW11 7BW, UK

The authorised representative in the EEA is Dorling Kindersley Verlag GmbH. Arnulfstr. 124, 80636 Munich, Germany

Published in the United States by DK Publishing, 1745 Broadway, 20th Floor, New York, NY 10019, USA

Copyright © 2005, 2023 Dorling Kindersley Limited A Penguin Random House Company

23 24 25 26 10 9 8 7 6 5 4 3 2

A CIP catalogue record is available from the British Library.

A catalogue record for this book is available from the Library of Congress.

ISSN 1479-344X

ISBN 978 0 2416 1535 5

Printed and bound in Malaysia www.dk.com

As a guide to abbreviations in visitor information blocks: **Adm** *= admission charge;* **D** *= dinner;* **L** *= lunch.*

MIX
Paper | Supporting responsible forestry
FSC™ C018179

This book was made with Forest Stewardship Council™ certified paper – one small step in DK's commitment to a sustainable future.
For more information go to www.dk.com/our-green-pledge

Phrase Book: Spanish

In an Emergency

Help!	¡Socorro!	soh-koh-roh
Stop!	¡Pare!	pah-reh
Call a doctor.	¡Llame a un médico!	yah-meh ah oon meh-de-koh
Call an ambulance.	¡Llame a una ambulancia!	yah-meh ah ahm-boo-lahn-thee-ah
Call the police	¡Llame a la policía!	yah-meh ah lah poh-lee-three-ah
Call the fire brigade.	¡Llame a los bomberos!	yah-meh ah lohs bohm-beh-rohs

Communication Essentials

Yes/No	Sí/No	see/noh
Please	Por favor	pohr fah-vorh
Thank you	Gracias	grah-thee-ahs
Excuse me	Perdone	pehr-doh-neh
Hello	Hola	oh-lah
Goodbye	Adiós	ah-dee-ohs
Good night	Buenas noches	bweh-nahs noh-chehs
What?	¿Qué?	keh?
When?	¿Cuándo?	kwan-doh?
Why?	¿Por qué?	pohr-keh?
Where?	¿Dónde?	dohn-deh?

Useful Phrases

How are you?	Cómo está usted?	koh-moh ehs-tah oos-tehd
Very well, thank you.	Muy bien, gracias.	mwee bee-ehn grah-thee-ahs
Pleased to meet you.	Encantado/a de conocerle.	ehn-kahn-tah-doh deh koh-noh-thehr-leh
That's fine.	Está bien.	ehs-tah bee-ehn
Where is/are …?	¿Dónde está/ están?	dohn-deh ehs-tah/ehs-tahn
Which way to …?	¿Por dónde se va a …?	pohr dohn-deh seh bah ah
Do you speak English?	¿Habla inglés?	ah-blah een-glehs
I don't understand.	No comprendo.	noh kom-prehn-doh
I'm sorry.	Lo siento.	loh see-ehn-toh

Shopping

How much does this cost?	¿Cuánto cuesta esto?	kwahn-toh kwehs-tah ehs-toh
I would like …	Me gustaría …	meh goos-ta-ree-ah
Do you have …?	¿Tienen …?	tee-yeh-nehn
Do you take credit cards?	¿Aceptan tarjetas de crédito?	ah-thehp-than tahr-heh-tas-deh kreh-deee-toh
What time do you open/ close?	A qué hora abren/cierran?	ah keh oh-rah ah-brehn/ thee-ehr-rahn
this one/ that one	éste/ése	ehs-teh/eh-seh
expensive	caro	kahr-oh
cheap	barato	bah-rah-toh
size (clothes)	talla	tah-yah
size (shoes)	número	noo-mehr-roh
white	blanco	blahn-koh
black	negro	neh-groh
red	rojo	roh-hoh
yellow	amarillo	ah-mah-ree-yoh
green	verde	behr-deh
blue	azul	ah-thool

Types of Shop

bakery	la panadería	lah pah-nah-deh-ree-ah
bank	el banco	ehl bahn-koh
bookshop	la librería	lah lee-breh-ree-ah
cake shop	la pastelería	lah pahs-teh-leh-ree-ah
chemist	la farmacia	lah fahr-mah-thee-ah
grocer's	la tienda de comestibles	lah tee-yehn-dah deh koh-mehs-tee-blehs
hairdresser	la peluquería	lah peh-loo-keh-ree-ah
market	el mercado	ehl mehr-kah-doh
newsagent	el kiosko de prensa	ehn kee-ohs-koh deh prehn-sah
supermarket	el super-mercado	ehl soo-pehr-mehr-kah-doh
travel agency	la agencia de viajes	lah ah-hehn-thee-ah deh bee-ah-hehs

Sightseeing

art gallery	la galería de arte	lah gah-leh-ree-ah deh ahr-teh
bus station	la estación de autobuses	lah ehs-tah-ee-ohn deh owtoh-boo-sehs
cathedral	la catedral	lah kah-teh-drahl
church	la iglesia/ la basílica	lah ee-gleh-see-ah/lah-bah-seel-i-kah
closed for holidays	cerrado por vacaciones	thehr-rah-doh porhr bah-kah-cee-oh-nehs
garden	el jardín	ehl hahr-deen
museum	el museo	ehl moo-seh-oh
railway station	la estación de trenes	lah ehs-tah-thee-ohn deh treh-nehs
tourist information	la oficina de turismo	lah oh-fee-thee-nah deh too-rees-moh

Staying in a Hotel

Do you have any vacant rooms?	¿Tienen una habitación libre?	tee-eh-nehn oo-nah ah-bee-tah thee-ohn lee-breh
double room	Habitación doble	ah-bee-tah-thee-ohn dob-bleh
with double bed	con cama de matrimonio	kohn kah-mah deh mah-tree-moh-nee-oh
twin room	Habitación con dos camas	ah-bee-tah-thee-ohn kohn dohs kah-mahs
single room	Habitación individual	ah-bee-tah-thee-ohn een-dee-vee-doo-ahl
room with a bath/shower	Habitación con baño/ducha	ah-bee-tah-thee-ohn kohn bah-nyoh/doo-chah
I have a reservation.	Tengo una habitación reservada.	tehn-goh oo-na ah-bee-tah-thee-ohn reh-sehr-bah-dah

Eating Out

Have you got a table for …?	¿Tienen mesa para …?	Tee-eh-nehn meh-sah pah-rah

I'd like to reserve a table.	Quiero reservar una mesa.	kee-eh-roh reh-sehr-bahr oo-nah meh-sah
breakfast	el desayuno	ehl deh-sah-yoo-noh
lunch	la comida/el almuerzo	lah koh-mee-dah/ehl ahl-mwehr-thoh
dinner	la cena	lah theh-nah
The bill, please.	La cuenta, por favor.	lah kwehn-tah pohr fah-vohr
waiter/waitress	camarero/ camarera	kah-mah-reh-roh/ kah-mah-reh-rah
fixed-price menu	menú del día	meh-noo dehl dee-ah
dish of the day	el plato del día	ehl plah-toh dehl dee-ah
starters	los entremeses	lohs ehn-treh-meh-sehs
main course	el primer plato	ehl pree-mehr plah-toh
wine list	la carta de vinos	lah kahr-tah deh bee-nohs
glass	un vaso	oon bah-soh
bottle	una botella	oon-nah boh-teh-yah
knife	un cuchillo	oon koo-chee-yoh
fork	un tenedor	oon the-neh-dohr
spoon	una cuchara	oon-ah koo-chah-rah
coffee	el café	ehl kah-feh
rare	poco hecho	poh-koh eh-choh
medium	medio hecho	meh-dee-oh eh-choh
well done	muy hecho	mwee eh-choh

Menu Decoder

al horno	ahl ohr-noh	baked
asado	ah-sah-do	roast
el aceite	ah-thee-eh-teh	oil
aceitunas	ah-theh-toon-ahs	olives
el agua mineral	ah-gwa mee-neh-rahl	mineral water
sin gas/con gas	seen gas/ kohn gas	still/sparkling
el ajo	ah-hoh	garlic
el arroz	ahr-rohth	rice
el azúcar	ah-thoo-kahr	sugar
la carne	kahr-ne	meat
la cebolla	theh-boh-yah	onion
la cerveza	thehr-beh-thah	beer
el cerdo	thehr-doh	pork
el chocolate	choh-koh-lah-the	chocolate
el chorizo	choh-ree-thoh	red sausage
el cordero	kohr-deh-roh	lamb
el fiambre	fee-ahm-breh	cold meat
frito	free-toh	fried
la fruta	froo-tah	fruit
los frutos secos	frooh-tohs seh-kohs	nuts
las gambas	gahm-bas	prawns
el helado	eh-lah-doh	ice cream
el huevo	oo-eh-voh	egg
el jamón serrano	hah-mohn sehr-rah-noh	cured ham
el jerez	heh-rehz	sherry
la langosta	lahn-gohs-tah	lobster
la leche	leh-cheh	milk
el limón	lee-mohn	lemon

la limonada	lee-moh-nah-dah	lemonade
la mantequilla	mahn-teh-kee-yah	butter
la manzana	mahn-thah-nah	apple
los mariscos	mah-rees-kohs	shellfish
la menestra	meh-nehs-trah	vegetable stew
la naranja	nah-rahn-hah	orange
el pan	pahn	bread
el pastel	pahs-tehl	cake
las patatas	pah-tah-thas	potatoes
el pescado	pehs-kah-doh	fish
la pimienta	pee-mee-yehn-tah	pepper
el plátano	plah-tah-noh	banana
el pollo	poh-yoh	chicken
el postre	pohs-treh	dessert
el queso	keh-soh	cheese
la sal	sahl	salt
las salchichas	sahl-chee-chahs	sausages
la salsa	sahl-sa	sauce
seco	seh-koh	dry
el solomillo	soh-loh-mee-yoh	sirloin
la sopa	soh-pah	soup
la tarta	tahr-ta	tart
el té	teh	tea
la ternera	tehr-neh-rah	beef
las tostadas	tohs-tah-dahs	toast
el vinagre	bee-nah-gre	vinegar
el vino blanco	bee-noh blahn-koh	white wine
el vino rosado	bee-noh roh-sah-doh	rosé wine
el vino tinto	bee-noh teen-toh	red wine

Numbers

0	cero	theh-roh
1	un/una	oon-noh/oon-uh
2	dos	dohs
3	tres	trehs
4	cuatro	kwa-troh
5	cinco	theen-koh
6	seis	says
7	siete	see-eh-teh
8	ocho	oh-choh
9	nueve	nweh-veh
10	diez	dee-ehth
11	once	ohn-theh
12	doce	doh-theh
13	trece	treh-theh
14	catorce	kah-tohr-theh
15	quince	keen-theh
16	dieciseis	dee-eh-thee-seh-ess
17	diecisiete	dee-eh-thee-see-eh-teh
18	dieciocho	dee-eh-thee-oh-choh
19	diecinueve	dee-eh-thee-newh-veh
20	veinte	beh-een-teh
30	treinta	treh-een-tah
40	cuarenta	kwah-rehn-tah
50	cincuenta	theen-kwehn-tah
60	sesenta	seh-sehn-tah
70	setenta	seh-tehn-tah
80	ochenta	oh-chehn-tah
90	noventa	noh-vehn-tah
100	cien	theh-ehn
1000	mil	meel
1001	mil uno	meel oo-noh

Phrase Book: Valencian

In an Emergency

Help!	Auxili!	ow-gzee-lee
Stop!	Pareu!	pah-reh-oo
Call a doctor!	Telefoneu un metge!	teh-leh-fon-eh-oo oom meh-djuh
Call an ambulance.	Telefoneu una ambulància!	teh-leh-fon-eh-oo oo-nah ahm-boo-lahn-see-ah
Call the police.	Telefoneu la policia!	teh-leh-fon-eh-oo lah poh-lee-see-ah
Call the fire brigade.	Telefoneu los bombers!	teh-leh-fon-eh-oo lohs bohm-behrs

Communication Essentials

Yes/No	Sí/No	see/noh
Please	Si us plau	si us plau
Thank you	Gràcies	grah-see-uhs
Excuse me	Perdoni	puhr-thoh-nee
Hello	Hola	oh-lah
Goodbye	Adéu	ah-they-oo
Good night	Bona nit	bo-nah neet
Yesterday	ahir	ah-ee
Today	avui	un-voo-ee
Tomorrow	demà	duh-mah
What?	Què?	keh?
When?	Quan?	kwahn
Why?	Per què?	puhr keh
Where?	On?	ohn

Useful Phrases

How are you?	Com està?	kom uhs-tah
Very well, thank you.	Molt bé, gràcies.	mol beh grah-see-uhs
Pleased to meet you.	Molt de gust.	mod duh goost
That's fine.	Està bé.	uhs-tah beh
Where is/are …?	On és/són …?	ohn ehs/sohn
Which way to …?	Per on es …?	puhr on uhs
Do you speak English?	Parla anglès?	par-luh an-glehs
I don't. understand	No l'entenc.	noh luhn-teng
I'm sorry.	Ho sento.	oo sehn-too

Shopping

How much does this cost?	Quant costa això?	kwahn kost ehs-shoh
I would like …	M'agradaría …	muh-grah-thuh-ree-ah
Do you have …?	Tenen …?	tehn-un
Do you take credit cards?	Accepten targetes de crèdit?	Ak-sehp-tuhn tahr-guh-tuhs duh kreh-deet
What time do you open/close?	A quina hora obren/ tanquen?	Ah keen-uh oh-bruhn/ tan-kuhn
this one/that one	aquest/aquell	Ah-ket/Ah-kehl
expensive	car	kahr
cheap	bé de preu/ barat	be thuh preh-oo/ bah-rat
size (clothes)	talla/mida	tah-lyah/mee-thuh
size (shoes)	número	noo-mehr-oo
white	blanc	blang
black	negre	neh-gruh
red	vermell	vuhr-mel
yellow	groc	grok
green	verd	behrt
blue	blau	blah-oo
bakery	el forn	uhl forn
bank	el banc	uhl bang

bookshop	la llibreria	lah lyee-burh-ree-ah
cake shop	la patisseria	lah pahs-tee-suh-ree-uh
chemist	la farmàcia	lah fuhr-mah-see-ah
grocer's	la botiga de queviures	lah boo-tee-guh duh kee-vee-oo-ruhs
hairdresser's	la perruqueria	lah peh-roo-kuh-ree-uh
market	el mercat	uhl mehr-kat
newsagent	el quiosc de premsa	uhl kee-ohsk duh prem-sah
supermarket	el supermercat	uhl soo-puhr-muhr-kat
travel agency	l'agència de viatges	la-jen-see-uh duh vee-ad-juhs

Sightseeing

art gallery	la galería d'art	lah gahl-luh-ree-yah dart
bus station	l'estació d' autobusos	luhs-tah-see-oh dow-toh-boo-zoos
cathedral	la catedral	lah kuh-tuh-thrahl
church	l'església/ la basílica	luhz-gleh-zee-uh/lah-buh-zee-lee-kuh
closed for holidays	tancat per vacances	tan-kat puhr bah-kan-suhs
garden	el jardí	uhl zhahr-dee
museum	el museu	uhl moo-seh-oo
railway station	l'estació de tren	luhs-tah-see-oh thuh tren
tourist information	l'oficina de turisme	loo-fee-see-nuh thuh too-reez-muh

Staying in a Hotel

Do you have any vacant rooms?	Tenen una habitació lliure?	teh-nuhn oo-nuh ah-bee-tuh-see oh lyuh-ruh
double room	habitació doble	ah-bee-tuh-see-oh doh-bluh
with double bed	amb llit de matrimoni	am lyeet duh mah-tree moh-nee
twin room	habitació amb dos llits/amb llits individuals	ah-bee-tuh-see-oh am dohs lyeets/am lyeets in-thee-vee-thoo-ahls
single room	habitació individual	ah-bee-tuh-see-oh in-thee-vee-thoo-ahl
room with a bath/shower	habitació amb bany/dutxa	ah-bee-tuh-see-oh am bahnyou/doo-chuh
I have a reservation.	Tinc una habitació reservada.	Ting oo-nuh ah-bee-tuh-see-oh reh-sehr-vah-thah

Eating Out

Have you got a table for …?	Tenen taula per …?	teh-nuhn tow-luh puhr
I'd like to reserve a table.	Voldria reservar una taula.	Vool-dree-uh reh-sehr-vahr oo-nuh tow-luh
breakfast	l'esmorzar	les-moor-sah
lunch	el dinar	uhl dee-nah
dinner	el sopar	uhl soo-pah

The bill, please.	el compte, si us plau.	uhl kohm-tuh sees plah-oo
waiter/waitress	cambrer/ cambrera	kam-breh/kam- breh-ruh
fixed-price menu	menú del dia	muh-noo thuhl dee-uh
dish of the day	el plat del dia	uhl plat duhl dee-uh
starters	els entrants	uhlz ehn-tranz
main course	el primer plat	uhl pree-meh plat
wine list	la carta de vins	lah kahr-tuh thuh veens
glass	un got	oon got
bottle	una ampolla	oo-nuh am-pol- yuh
knife	un ganivet	oon gun-ee- veht
fork	una forquilla	oo-nuh foor- keel-yuh
spoon	una cullera	oo-nuh kool- yeh-ruh
coffee	el café	ehl kah-feh
rare	poc fet	pok fet
medium	al punt	ahl poon
well done	molt fet	mol fet

Menu Decoder

l'aigua mineral	lah-ee-gwuhl mee-nuh-rah	mineral water
sense gas/ amb gas	sen-zuh gas/ am gas	still/ sparkling
l'all	lahlyuh	garlic
al forn	ahl forn	roasted
l'arròs	lahr-roz	rice
les botifarres	lahs boo-tee- fah-rahs	cured meats
la carn	lah karn	meat
la ceba	lah seh-buh	onion
la cervesa	lah-sehr-ve-seh	beer
el filet	uhl fee-let	sirloin
el formatge	uhl for- mah-djuh	cheese
l'embotit	lum-boo-teet	cold meat
fregit	freh-zeet	fried
la fruita	lah froo-ee-tah	fruit
els fruits secs	uhlz froo- eets seks	nuts
les gambes	lahs gam-bus	prawns
el gelat	uhl djuh-lat	ice-cream
la llagosta	lah lyah-gos-tah	lobster
la llet	lah lyet	milk
la llimona	lah lyee- moh-nah	lemon
la llimonada	lah lyee-moh- nah-thuh	lemonade
la mantega	lah mahn- teh-gah	butter
el marisc	ulh mur-reesk	seafood
la menestra	lah muh- nehs-truh	vegetable stew
el pa	uhl pah	bread
el pastís	uhl pahs-tees	pie/cake
les patates	lahs pah- tah-tuhs	potatoes
el peix	pehs-kah-doh	fish
el pebre	pee-mee- yehn-tah	pepper
el pernil	uhl puhr-neel	cured ham
el plàtan	uhl plah-tan	banana
el pollastre	uhl puu- lyah-struh	chicken
la poma	lah poh-mah	apple
el porc	uhl pohr	pork
les postres	lahs pohs-truhs	desserts
rostit	rohs-teet	roast
la sal	lah sahl	salt
les salsitxes	lahs sahl- see-chuhs	sausages
la salsa	lah sahl-suh	sauce

sec	sehk	dry
el sucre	uhl soo-kruh	sugar
la taronja	lah tuh- rohn-djuh	orange
el te	uhl teh	tea
les torrades	lahs too- rah-thuhs	toast
la vedella	lah veh- theh-lyuh	beef
el vi blanc	uhl bee blang	white wine
el vi negre	uhl bee neh-greh	red wine
el vi rosat	uhl bee roo-zaht	rosé wine
el xai/el be	uhl shahee/ uhl beh	lamb
la xocolata	lah shoo- koo-lah-tuh	chocolate

Numbers

0	zero	zeh-roh
1	un/una	oon/oon-uh
2	dos/dues	dohs/doo-uhs
3	tres	trehs
4	quatre	kwa-truh
5	cinc	seeng
6	sis	sees
7	set	set
8	vuit	voo-eet
9	nou	noh-oo
10	deu	deh-oo
11	onze	on-zuh
12	dotze	doh-dzuh
13	tretze	treh-dzuh
14	catorze	kah-tohr-dzuh
15	quinze	keen-zuh
16	setze	set-zuh
17	disset	dee-set
18	divuit	dee-voo-eet
19	dinou	dee-noh-oo
20	vint	been
21	vint-i-un	been-tee-oon
30	trenta	tren-tah
40	quaranta	kwuh-ran-tuh
50	cinquanta	seen-kwahn-tah
60	seixanta	seh-ee-shan-tah
70	setanta	seh-tan-tah
80	viutanta	voo-ee-tan-tah
90	noranta	noh-ran-tah
100	cent	sen
101	cent un	sen oon
1000	mil	meel
1001	mil un	meel oo-noh

The following words crop up frequently in maps and on street signs. You may encounter them in their Spanish or Valencian forms, depending on which part of the Costa Blanca you are visiting.

English	Spanish	Valencian
Avenue	Avenida	Avinguda
Beach	Playa	Platja
Cape	Cabo	Cap
Castle	Castillo	Castell
Market	Mercado	Mercat
Museum	Museo	Museu
Square	Plaza	Plaça
Street	Calle	Carrer
Town Hall	Ayuntamiento	Ajuntament

Selected Sight Index